Elizabeth Johnson

Questing for God

Heidi Schlumpf

LITURGICAL PRESS
Collegeville, Minnesota

www.litpress.org

1	2	3	4	5	6	7	8	9

Library of Congress Control Number: 2015957676

ISBN 978-0-8146-4817-9   978-0-8146-4842-1 (ebook)

For my parents,
Ed and Mary Schlumpf,
who inspired my Catholicism,
my feminism,
and my love of writing—
all of which come together in this book.

Contents

Acknowledgments   ix

Introduction   1

Chapter One
Eldest Child: Growing Up in Brooklyn   11

Chapter Two
Young Nun: Becoming a Sister of St. Joseph   22

Chapter Three
Budding Scholar: Teaching and Learning
after Vatican II   34

Chapter Four
Awakened Feminist: Finding Her Voice at CUA   47

Chapter Five
Disciplined Writer: Sharing with the World   64

Chapter Six
Caring Teacher: Mentoring Students at Fordham   79

Chapter Seven
Public Intellectual: Handling Controversy
with Grace   95

Epilogue   113

Notes   123

Bibliography   135

Index   138

Acknowledgments

Although I have loved writing this book, it was not my idea. That honor belongs to the wise folks at Liturgical Press, who conceived the People of God series of inspirational biographies and thought fit to fairly represent women authors and subjects. I am grateful to publisher Barry M. Hudock for asking me to contribute to the series—and for the idea of writing about Elizabeth Johnson. Managing editor J. Andrew Edwards has carefully shepherded the project, with the help of very competent copyeditors, proofreaders, designers, and marketers.

I am also indebted to the authors of previous volumes in this series who have modeled how to write a compelling, popular biography. Sister Rose Pacatte, SP (*Martin Sheen: Pilgrim on the Way*), gave tips on research, while Kevin Clarke (*Oscar Romero: Love Must Win Out*) reminded me not to bury the lead.

In researching Johnson's life, I was greatly assisted by the helpful staff at the University of Notre Dame Archives, where her personal and professional papers are housed, and by Johnson's friends, family, and colleagues who consented to in-person or telephone interviews.

Two people immensely improved upon my first draft of this manuscript: Heather Grennan Gary, a former colleague and friend, did amazing edits, as did my sister Amy Schlumpf Manion, who is a first-rate proofreader. Both read and edited the manuscript under a very tight deadline, for which I (and my editors, I'm sure) are so grateful. Any errors in the final book, however, are mine.

A biographer is not supposed to fall in love with her subject, but when your subject is Beth Johnson, it's nearly impossible not to. Before writing this book, I knew Beth only through her work, though I must have met her at least once, as I owned a signed copy of *She Who Is*. She is not someone who enjoys the limelight, so I am grateful that she consented to the project and was so open with me throughout my year of research and writing. She also is the most organized person I have ever met, which is extremely helpful when you're trying to gather and sift through a life's worth of information. Above all, she is kind and caring—this, on top of being one of the most astute and creative theological minds of our generation. I am honored to write about her life.

Finally, this book could not have been written without the patience of my colleagues and other editors, especially as this manuscript's deadline approached, and the support of my husband, Edmund, who kept our children, Sam and Sophie, occupied while Mama was writing all summer. For all who helped birth this book—and, of course, to the Living God, "She Who Is"—who is the source of everything, I am deeply grateful.

Heidi Schlumpf

Introduction

During the busiest season of the academic year, just days before the pinnacle that is commencement, the three dozen members of the theology faculty at Fordham University set aside their grading of final exams and other end-of-the-year administrative tasks for an annual daylong retreat. The idea is to reflect and dream, not to consider specific proposals but rather to brainstorm how to make one of the strongest Catholic theology departments in the country even better. Some still refer to the day as "Mitchell Farm," since it used to be held at a villa in the Hudson Valley that had been donated to the Jesuits. But after the order sold that property, the retreat day was moved to Fordham's Westchester campus in West Harrison, New York, which houses the university's graduate and professional programs. It is a less bucolic site but still remote enough that faculty will not be tempted to scurry back to their offices or meet with students.

The day begins with prayer and ends with a cocktail party and dinner. Faculty members bring their own specialties; the homemade guacamole made by one professor being particularly popular. But before drinks are served, they gather for a final, vespers-like prayer service to conclude their day's work. The Westchester campus chapel is too small

1

to hold them all, so a classroom is turned into a makeshift sacred space. The service, planned by a committee of faculty members, begins with music, includes readings from Scripture, and ends with petitionary prayers that mention any deaths or births that have touched members of the department during the past school year. It is a rare opportunity for these academics, who talk theology all day, to pray together and witness one another's spirituality in a less academic setting.

In May 2011, toward the end of that year's prayer service, a lector began reading a beautiful litany of names for God: Gracious Mystery, Holy Wisdom, Divine Presence, The God Who Accompanies, Ground of Our Being, A Bountiful God. As the names were recited, one faculty member, Sr. Elizabeth Johnson, smiled with knowing recognition. The names had been culled from Johnson's book, *Quest for the Living God: Mapping Frontiers in the Theology of God*, which six weeks earlier had been publicly rebuked by the US bishops' Committee on Doctrine. Although the members of Fordham's faculty had already expressed solidarity with their colleague in various ways—signing statements of support, speaking out in the media, offering comfort and advice—this gesture was perhaps the most poignant. As the many names for God were spoken, Johnson was touched by what was clearly meant as a tribute, but even more importantly, she was struck by the magnificence of the rich theology being done in the church today that those names represented—exactly what she had tried to capture in the book. "It was a real moment of grace," she recalls.

At the time, Johnson was still embroiled in the controversy that would make her something of a cause célèbre among Catholics, an individual symbol in what came to be seen as part of a larger, unfair attack on women religious in

America in the new millennium. It started in 2008, when the Vatican's Congregation for Institutes of Consecrated Life and Societies of Apostolic Life initiated an apostolic visitation of the four hundred non-cloistered communities of religious women in the United States out of concern for "the welfare of religious women and consecrated life in general."[1] After the visitation's final report in 2014, another Vatican office, the Congregation for the Doctrine of the Faith (CDF), began a "doctrinal assessment" of a group of US women's congregations, the Leadership Conference of Women Religious (LCWR), saying it suspected "dissent" and "doctrinal confusion" on the part of that organization.[2] In the midst of those two headline-producing controversies, the US bishops' committee issued a public criticism of perhaps the most prominent woman religious theologian in the country. All three backfired, at least on the public relations front, with American Catholics rallying to support the beloved sisters who had taught them in their youth and who were seen, in contrast to the male hierarchy, as embodying the best of Christianity in the way they lived out the gospel message of Jesus.

At the time of the retreat prayer service in 2011, Johnson was in the middle of writing what would be a thirty-eight-page response to the bishops' criticism of her book—a response they requested but ultimately would ignore in their "response to her response." She was physically and mentally exhausted, and somewhat spiritually wounded, by the whole ordeal, which had started at the end of March. Still, she was looking forward with enthusiasm to a planned sabbatical the next school year, during which she would put Thomas Aquinas and Charles Darwin in conversation to explore how theology could better respond to the ecological crisis facing the earth. The litany at the retreat prayer service reminded her of the joy she found in what has been her life's work: to wrestle with the mystery that is God, especially in the context of the experience of Catholics in the late twentieth and early twenty-first centuries.

That is Johnson's quest, and, despite the hurdles she has faced in her decades of trying to understand God, it is an assignment Johnson has willingly and happily embraced. "To me, it's a spiritual adventure," she says, explaining why she chose the word *quest* for her book's title. "We're never going to capture the fullness of God. God is still going to be greater than all of us."

While such a journey is the responsibility of every human being, it is the particular task of the theologian to ask the questions pertinent to his or her age. Johnson draws on her beloved Karl Rahner, a German priest and theologian who influenced the Second Vatican Council, in seeing questioning as one of a theologian's vital activities. "The day we stop questioning is the day we're dead," she says. "We have an infinite number of questions in us to ask, and each one is implicitly orienting us to the truth, the beautiful, and the good that is God."

At seventy-four, Johnson has lived through times in the church when questioning was suppressed, then encouraged, and once again suppressed. Throughout it all, she has stuck to her belief that theology is not only "faith seeking understanding," as St. Anselm put it in the eleventh century, but "love seeking understanding," as she has put it in the twenty-first. To her, God must be the "living God" mentioned in the Scriptures, most notably in the Psalms and the books of the prophets. The term, to her, means "a sense of the God who is full of energy and spirit, alive with designs for liberation and healing, always approaching from the future to do something new,"[3] as she writes in the introduction to *Quest for the Living God*. The living God is the God of flowing water and wind, the God of justice, and the God of love.

It is this groundedness in the living God and in God's mystery that has sustained Johnson during difficult times: at the death of her father after her high school graduation, in her twenties when she struggled with pre-Vatican II religious life, after Vatican II as one of the first women to earn a doctorate in theology at the Catholic University of America and the first tenure-track woman professor of theology there, during her heated battle for tenure at CUA, and finally during the criticism of *Quest for the Living God* and subsequent controversy over being given LCWR's Outstanding Leadership Award in 2014.

In one of her first public talks, as commencement speaker at St. Joseph Academy in New York in 1980, Johnson laid out her belief in God's mysterious goodness. "In real life, the future breaks into every life in ways that are startling and strange. Sometimes it comes creatively, filled with new possibilities. Sometimes it brings destruction, and ruins what we love," she said. "But what will last is *life,* transformation, happiness beyond our wildest imaginings. . . . No situation is so desperate, no person so broken, that God cannot arrive with an entirely new possibility for an even greater future."[4]

Yet when asked to describe her personal spirituality, Johnson is reticent and at something of a loss for words. As a child growing up in Brooklyn, she was in love with the prayers and devotions of the pre-Vatican II church. Similarly, the Ignatian *examen* and daily Mass were a part of her life as a sister for decades. Today, however, she is careful to attend a parish where she can be an anonymous member of the community. She used to listen to a radio program every Friday afternoon at five o'clock that broadcast the Sabbath service from Temple Emmanuel in New York City, and she would pray along with the *Kaddish* prayer for the dead. Johnson admits she finds Judaism appealing. "So much of Christianity is taken from Judaism: God acting in history, the presence of the Spirit, the call to be honest and care for the neighbor," she says. "Jesus gave it a new kind of life in the Gentile world, but the heart of it is very Jewish."

Jesus is important to her faith, of course, and so is Mary, but she is not one for typical Catholic devotions at this point in her life. The closest she gets to a daily ritual is to get up each morning and make a cup of tea, light a candle, and pray for a while, usually with the Scriptures. Mark is her favorite gospel, because of the simplicity of the narrative, and she loves the Psalms and Wisdom literature of the Hebrew Scriptures. When praying, she avoids reading commentaries and other books so she can "turn off the thinking." She says she finds the Bible refreshing. "I can go for days at a time praying with just a phrase of Scripture," she says. "It's disastrous if I start reading. Then my theological side kicks in."

Her image of God is fundamentally trinitarian, tending to emphasize the Spirit as the presence and action of God in the world. She is "of the world," but not worldly, caring little about money or material possessions. All of her book royalties, speaking honorariums, and prize monies—as well as her salary—go directly to the Sisters of St. Joseph of Brentwood, her religious congregation. Her clothes are professional looking, but after a while, it is easy to tell from the rotation of outfits that she doesn't have a lot of them. Although she lives simply, she has no interest in being cloistered and believes it is her task to challenge people to think about God in such a way that it affects how they act in the world.

As a teacher and writer, she works with words, but she eschews words when she prays. "I love to be in communion with God, without a whole lot of talking going on," she explains. Her goal is to "be in God's presence," which can happen in a variety of ways, including in nature. She lives near a lake and frequently takes walks around it. Each summer she reconnects and rejuvenates with a week or two at the family cottage on the Atlantic Ocean. But she also learned from the writings of Dietrich Bonhoeffer, the German Lutheran pastor executed by the Nazis, that God wants Christians to be out in the world where the suffering is. For her, that means she can experience God while washing her windows or sitting with a student—and she doesn't have to be explicitly thinking about God while she's doing it for it to be holy.

In the 1960s, reading Bonhoeffer's letters written from prison—and French Jesuit philosopher Pierre Teilhard de Chardin—helped Johnson let go of a neoscholastic understanding of God as a rule-oriented judge or monarch, a release she found liberating. Bonhoeffer wrote: "Before God and with God we live without God"—a phrase Johnson says she put on a banner when she was young and "in the banner making stage."[5] To her, it means God is beyond humans' complete understanding, but God touches people so they can get on with the business of serving the world and those in need. She calls it a "holy secularity," which doesn't deny the existence of God but neither requires constant overt religiosity to acknowledge God's connection to creation.

Her deepest experience of God is as "Infinite Holy Mystery," a phrase from Rahner that emphasizes that the Divine is beyond all imagination. Yet, ironically, her life's task has been to wrestle with who this ineffable God is and to help others recognize that the way we imagine and talk about God matters. Ultimately, to understand Johnson's spirituality, you must go to her work. That is where she has worked out who God is, what God means in her life, and what the ramifications are of that God for the church and for the world.

Her early theological work began in Christology, sparked perhaps by her own experiences of suffering, including the tragic loss of her father. Her senior thesis in college was on the resurrection, and her first paper submitted to (and rejected by) an academic journal was about freedom and the book of Job. In her graduate studies, Johnson quickly found herself interested in language about God. Her doctoral dissertation studied a Protestant, German theologian (Wolfhart Pannenberg) whose work on the resurrection intrigued her, but she also ended up analyzing the use of analogy in the way Christians speak about God.

Johnson's first book, *Consider Jesus: Waves of Renewal in Christology*, was a Christology primer, but her first real work of theology looked at language about God in a feminist context. *She Who Is: The Mystery of God in Feminist Theological Discourse*, which proposed reclaiming feminine images of the Divine, was perhaps Johnson's best-known work before the bishops' investigation of *Quest for the Living God*. Her love of the Catholic tradition led her to try to reimagine Mariology in *Truly Our Sister: A Theology of Mary in the Communion of Saints* and the communion of saints in *Friends of God and Prophets: A Feminist Theological Reading of the Communion of Saints*, while her most recent book, *Ask the Beasts: Darwin and the God of Love*, is about theological implications on the environmental crisis. There is hardly an aspect of systematic theology she has not written about, but throughout it all, the key issue is God. "Is God a mystery beyond all comprehension, and if so what is the nature of our language about that?" she asks.

Despite the seriousness of those topics, Johnson is surprisingly personable, even nice. Colleagues and students say she can be "mom-like," and they mean that in both a positive and negative sense. She'll give a student chocolate when one is feeling down, but still give the D she or he deserves on a poorly written paper. She is extraordinarily prolific and productive, in part because her choice of religious life means she has no spouse or children to care for. But she serves as the matriarch of her extended family, the one who keeps track of all the birthdays and organizes the annual Thanksgiving get-together. She likes to cook, loves her cat, and enjoys the symphony.

In all things, Johnson is disciplined. Her papers, recently donated to the University of Notre Dame archives, are amazingly organized, each file folder labeled with her perfect penmanship, nearly every card and letter she's ever received carefully saved and cataloged by her. She has a sense of humor, but overall she is quite serious, especially about her work. She takes criticism, from fellow academics and even from students, but not if it misinterprets her thinking. Johnson can be single-mindedly focused. A friend remembers her working on a paper in graduate school, a note pinned to the curtain next to her desk reminding her to get a rare criticism from a professor out of her mind. She went on to write an A paper.

She is known worldwide and likely to be remembered as one of the most prominent and influential theologians of her generation. Yet, the prominence, the awards, the hundreds of requests to speak, and other accolades have not gone to her head. She's somewhat embarrassed by attention to her personally; she'd much rather people would talk about her work than about her life. When two colleagues put together a book called *Things New and Old: Essays on the Theology of Elizabeth A. Johnson*, in which other scholars reflected on her work, she was moved and humbled.

In her own contribution to that book, she wrote that it had been an "inestimable privilege" to be engaged in the "intellectual adventure" of theological work with so many fine colleagues. Yet she acknowledged that, whatever her contributions, they pale in comparison to the wondrous mystery of God, writing, "Just let my tombstone read: 'She lost as gracefully as possible in the effort to understand God for the sake of resisting evil and healing the world.' "[6]

CHAPTER ONE

Eldest Child

Growing Up in Brooklyn

Giggles erupt as the players in the annual Christmas pageant take their places "on stage" in the crowded living room of the attached brownstone on Sixty-First Street in Brooklyn. The Johnson family's seven children—all about a year and a half apart plus some neighborhood kids—mean enough cast members for two angels, three innkeepers, and one shepherd. That leaves the writing, directing, and narrating of this five-scene production, as usual, to the eldest child, Elizabeth or "Beth."[1]

Beth was always making up games for her six siblings—postdinner games of softball and "I declare war on . . ." or "I see the color of . . ."—or staging plays that involved the whole neighborhood. As the oldest, she was responsible for her younger siblings, but she made chores fun by incorporating singing into them. "She was a natural leader," remembers her sister Dr. Margaret "Peggy" Johnson Bia. "Beth was always very no-nonsense, purposeful, somewhat on the serious side, as opposed to frivolous. But she always had self-confidence."

Peggy is the youngest of the four oldest girls; next came their brother ("He got treated like a royal prince," Beth remembers), and finally the last two girls. The Johnson home was small—with three or four kids to a bedroom, only a bath and a half, and little yard to speak of—so creativity was required to keep seven kids occupied and happy while stuck indoors. Squabbles weren't uncommon. Every Sunday night was the family "council of war," in which each child was allowed one complaint that the parents would negotiate. "The fact they called it the 'council of war' tells you everything," says Susan Johnson, the second youngest.

Although she was nine years younger, Susan saw her eldest sister, Beth, as an ally she could count on. Once, when she was five or six, Susan captured a dozen caterpillars and put them in a peanut butter jar with holes in the top. Later that night, she was overtaken by guilt and determined to free the little critters, although she didn't dare break the rules by getting out of bed after lights out. "I thought of all the people who could help me liberate those caterpillars, it was Beth," she says. The two sneaked outside and let the insects go.

Beth is simultaneously remembered as the leader of childhood fun but also as hyper-responsible and always having her nose in a book. While she was reading *Heidi*, she taught her siblings to drink milk out of a bowl and eat cheese like the main character.[2] Imaginative yet disciplined, she was influenced by several strong women in her life, including her mother and an aunt. "Our Irish family was the scene of frequent lively debates (usually revolving around politics) and as children we were encouraged to participate," she wrote in a statement for a graduate school scholarship.[3] As a young girl, Beth would set her alarm clock and make the four-block uphill climb to the parish church for daily Mass, so no one was surprised when she entered the convent after high school. For the most part her childhood mirrored that of most Irish Catholic families of that generation; Beth remembers growing up in a happy home filled with family, unconditional love, and faith.

Elizabeth Ann Johnson came into the world on St. Nicholas Day, December 6, 1941, less than twenty-four hours before the attack on Pearl Harbor. Born at St. Mary's Hospital in Brooklyn, she was named for "The Blessed Mother's mother and cousin,"[4] according to her baby book, which is as detailed as only a first child's can be. It is recorded that Beth spoke her first word on July 15, 1942, for example, and her first outing was on January 1, 1942, when she went "for a ride in the auto along Shore Road and Belt Parkway in Brooklyn."[5] The healthy but bald baby was baptized two weeks after her birth at Our Lady of Perpetual Help Parish on Fifth Avenue between Fifty-Ninth and Sixtieth Streets in the Sunset Park neighborhood.

Her father, Walter Johnson, was working as an insurance broker when his first child was born, but eventually became a safety inspector for American Airlines at LaGuardia Airport. (He later returned to the insurance business.) One of thirteen children, Walter had five brothers, all of whom would serve in World War II, though Walter did not, since the airline needed him for domestic flights at home.

Johnson has fond memories of her father, including a visit to the airport that included a chance to walk up the steps to a plane—thrilling to the then seven-year-old. His bedtime stories, told as bribes to get his children to go to sleep, included tales of how Oklahoma oil wells looked like Christmas trees from the window of an airplane. Every Father's Day he would go on retreat to Mount Manresa, a Jesuit retreat house on Staten Island, and his children would tuck handmade cards and gifts in his suitcase before he left. Beth always asked him to bring her back some specimens for her leaf collection. As the oldest, Beth had a closer relationship with her father than the other children had, her siblings remember.

Walter Johnson was a native of Brooklyn; his parents, Thomas and Loretto, owned the brownstone where Beth grew up, and her grandparents lived upstairs. Walter's was a religious family, according to an article written on the occasion of his parents' fiftieth wedding anniversary by their daughter Virginia Therese Johnson, a Maryknoll sister. Beth's paternal grandparents had married in 1912; Thomas worked two jobs, in a controller's office and at the post office, so the children could have piano and violin lessons and go to summer camps, Niagara Falls, and Washington, DC. "The mother bought almost every juvenile book sold in the religious goods stores on Barclay Street in Manhattan for the home library,"[6] recalled the Maryknoll daughter. She also remembered daily recitation of the rosary, the singing of hymns to the Sacred Heart and Blessed Mother, and a large home altar with statues of each child's patron saint. Both parents were daily communicants, and priests were frequent dinner guests. Of the six girls in the family, five entered religious life, including two to the order their niece would later join.[7]

As one of thirty-six grandchildren to her paternal grandparents, young Beth was not as close to them as she was to her mother's side of the family. Her mother, Margaret Reed Johnson, was born in Massachusetts, but grew up in Brooklyn after her father moved the family to the city to find a job during the Depression. Margaret's father's ancestors came over on the Mayflower, while her mother was the child of Irish immigrants. The Protestant, blue-blooded Reed family opposed the marriage.

Beth remembers her maternal grandmother, Mary Agnes Donovan Reed, who went by Agnes, as "full of spunk." After graduating from high school, she worked as a secretary, and her first purchase with her earnings was rather luxurious and impractical: a boat. "She was full of songs and music and poetry," Johnson says. She even penned a poem about her first grandchild:

> She doesn't hide her light under a bushel,
> She lets it shine where're it can,
> No child could give more satisfaction than clever
>   Elizabeth Ann.[8]

Frescos painted by Johnson's grandmother still decorated the walls of the family home in Westchester County when Margaret's sister, Barbara, lived there after their parents' deaths. As a child, visits to Beth's grandparents' home in the country, with its large yard, were fun, and rides on her grandparents' boat a welcome respite from the city.

Aunt Barbara Reed, Johnson's godmother, was a special influence and would remain an important part of her life even past the death of her parents. Unmarried with no children of her own, Reed worked for AIG, the insurance company, and used some of her salary to spoil her goddaughter with treats. She would buy pretty dresses for her on her birthday and take her to restaurants or Coney Island. Johnson still has the gold cross her Aunt Barbara gave her on her baptism. A later baby photo of Beth depicts her with a few damp curls, a dress embroidered with flowers, and the gold cross around her neck and a gold ring on her middle left finger.[9] The ring also was a gift from Aunt Barbara and has been passed down to Beth's eldest niece.

Johnson's maternal grandmother, aunt, and her mother were strong women who clearly influenced young Beth, although they would not have been called feminists at the time.

"They lived their lives the way they wanted to, being loving, strong and faithful," Johnson recalls. "They were just being who they were." The Johnson daughters include a nurse, a physician/professor at Yale Medical School, the CEO of a large hospice corporation, and, of course, a prominent theologian. When people would ask their mother how she had such successful daughters, she would say, "I have no idea. I had nothing to do with it." But of course she was a role model, Peggy remembers. "She wouldn't go out marching with Betty Friedan, but she was a very strong woman. She didn't want to talk about women's lib or anything. Yet she was out there living it."

Although she worked as a homemaker after she married, Johnson's mother had graduated from Hunter College with a degree in mathematics. Education was highly valued and expected of all the Johnson children, regardless of gender. Young Beth was a model student at Our Lady of Perpetual Help School (OLPH), which was divided by gender, so for all intents and purposes an all-girls school. Those early experiences in a single-gender environment may have contributed to Johnson's leadership qualities. "There was a lot of emphasis on learning, getting good grades, achieving," she recalls. On report card day, if all the children in the family had passed their subjects, their father would buy a gallon of ice cream as a treat. Johnson remembers her mother saying, "Not everyone has to get an A. You just have to do your best and pass."

Johnson did more than just pass. An early report card from 1951 is decorated with five gold stars. Johnson earned all high As, except for an 85 in penmanship, which she brought up to a 91 by the spring term. She received 100s in religion. Although she had a few absences, she was never late and had no absences for Mass.[10] At her eighth-grade graduation in 1955, Johnson received a gold medal and ten dollars for first prize in religion.[11] She had gotten glasses at a young age, and her family teased her that she was going blind from reading so much. "She was an avid reader, always looking things up," recalls Peggy. "Every place you went, Beth was buried in a book."

Our Lady of Perpetual Help Parish was founded and run by Redemptorist priests and served predominantly Irish families. The large stone church, now a basilica, sits atop a hill and can be seen from quite a distance, including from the Narrows harbor. The artwork in the church was traditional, as were the pre-Second Vatican Council devotions. This was the parish where Johnson first received the sacraments of communion and reconciliation. As a young girl, she recalls marching her siblings up the hill on All Souls' Day to earn plenary indulgences for saying six "Our Fathers," "Hail Marys," or "Glory Bes." Although her friends still kid her about the practice, Johnson saw it as an important lesson in being oriented toward others. "The sisters told me that I could get a soul out of purgatory. That was a lot of power to put in the hands of a ten-year-old girl—affecting someone's eternal salvation," she says. "I took it seriously."

Of course, the Sisters of St. Joseph who taught at the school were also planting the idea of a religious vocation in the minds and hearts of their students. Johnson remembers the sisters as excellent teachers. "We never had that hitting your hands with the rulers. It was just concentrated, good teaching. They really wanted you to understand the material," she says. The annual vocation talk from Sr. Margaret Andre was a welcome break from regular classes, but also painted an attractive vision of a life spent loving God. It didn't hurt that the young nun was one of the girls' favorites, a kind, funny woman who seemed to enjoy her life in the convent.

Johnson was among nine girls from OLPH who earned entrance into St. Brendan's Diocesan High School for Girls in the Midwood neighborhood of Brooklyn, where she would continue her academic success and discover her own intellectual bent. Studying French, algebra, and world history made for four glorious years of learning. "I would just eat it up," she remembers. Her leadership skills also were groomed in high school: she served as editor of the school newspaper and president of the Glee Club, performing in concerts and learning to dance the Charleston.

Although she was one of the smartest girls in the school, Johnson wasn't competitive or proud, according to childhood friend Jean Hostetter Ramierez. "She did her best because that's what you do. She used her gifts, but she didn't lord it over other people," recalls Ramierez, who believes her friend accepted her intelligence as a fact of life and gift from God.

At St. Brendan, Johnson and Ramierez were part of a group of five friends from the academic side of the high school (it also had a commercial side for young women not planning on college). They were all good students, more focused on choosing a good university than finding a husband. Ramierez remembers going to dances and out for sodas at Hinsches ice cream shop. She also accompanied the Johnson family to their summer bungalow in the Rockaways at Breezy Point, where she got a taste of life in a big family. At some point, someone started calling Beth Johnson and Jean Hostetter the "Johnstetter twins," even though they look nothing alike, and the nickname stuck. The two are still close today.

Three of that group of five young women entered religious life; in addition to Beth, two joined the order affiliated with the Missionary Cenacle Apostolate, a lay Catholic organization founded in the early twentieth century by a priest in

New York. Johnson and her friends had become involved
with the apostolate through volunteer work at the Henry
Street Settlement House near the Brooklyn Bridge. As part
of the Student Service League, the young women tutored
African American and Puerto Rican children from nearby
housing projects. Johnson remembers being "floored" by
the poverty, compared to the relative wealth of her working-
class neighborhood.

Another memory emphasizes how Johnson's parents
taught their children to respect others who were different.
One year the family piled into the station wagon to go to
the Chinese New Year parade in Manhattan. As they got
close to Chinatown, one of the kids started laughing at
a man with long, black braids walking down the street.
Johnson's mother turned to the back seat and scolded:
"Don't you dare ever do that! God created them in his image
and likeness, just the same as you. They're God's children."
Johnson remembers not only the colored paper dragons
from that day, but her mother's anger. "She hardly ever got
mad, so when she did, it made an impression."

Decades later, after Johnson's mother's death in 2002,
Aunt Barbara would take over as the matriarch in the family. As her godmother aged, Beth picked up the responsibility. All six of her siblings married, and she is an aunt to
eleven nieces and nephews and great-aunt to twelve grand-
nieces and grandnephews. She is the one who keeps track
of everyone's address, email, and phone number, updating
a family document annually and sharing it.

She also has become the organizer of the annual Thanksgiving dinner, one of two holidays the whole family tries to
celebrate together (the other is the Fourth of July). Tradi-
tionally, Aunt Barbara had always organized the holiday,
but gradually Beth took over, assigning siblings a dish to

bring and asking everyone to email her the things for which they are grateful that year. Rather than go around the table and share gratitude, which was always interspersed with giggles, the practice of writing them out beforehand gives family members time to write deeper reflections, which Beth reads before dinner. When Aunt Barbara became too ill to host, Beth secured a nearby Boy Scout cabin large enough to hold the whole clan. In 2014, thirty-five members of the family, including Aunt Barbara in a wheelchair, gathered in the cabin, with its big, roaring fireplace, to give thanks.

After her Aunt Barbara had a stroke in 2013, Beth found herself taking care of her godmother, rather than the other way around. Her aunt lived not far from Johnson, who did her grocery shopping, arranged for a hospital bed, and handled all the other details of caring for an aging family member. In 2015, the family decided she needed an assisted living facility, which Beth, who holds power of attorney, also spearheaded. (Aunt Barbara died in October 2015.) "Everyone in the family pitches in," Johnson notes. But as the eldest, she is the coordinator.

Back in the spring of 1959, as high school graduation for the eldest Johnson child approached, she continued to accumulate academic awards, including honors in Latin and French, a certificate of superior merit for proficiency in Latin, membership in the Leo Honor Society, and a National Merit Scholarship. She would earn three college scholarships: to St. John's University in New York, Wilmington College in Ohio, and the University of the State of New York Regents Scholarship, the latter garnering a letter from the president of the Borough of Brooklyn congratulating her for proving "once again that our Brooklyn students are second to none in the entire United States."[12]

Johnson would not end up using any of those college scholarships. She had already made up her mind to enter the convent of the religious women who had taught at her elementary and high school, the Sisters of St. Joseph of Brentwood. She was ready to make the move toward religious life, but one thing almost stopped her. One rainy morning, on the way to his job at an insurance company on Wall Street, her father slipped on the stairs to the subway and fractured his skull. He was rushed to the hospital, where he underwent brain surgery for a blood clot. There, he caught meningitis and died. He was forty-four and left a wife and seven children. The eldest, Beth, was just seventeen.

CHAPTER TWO

Young Nun

Becoming a Sister of St. Joseph

The Johnson family was in collective shock that summer of 1959; Walter Johnson had gone to work one July day and had never come home. Susan Johnson, who was eight at the time, was convinced her father hadn't really died and was hiding in a closet in the basement. Beth Johnson remembers being "catatonic with grief." She had just graduated from high school and was scheduled to enter the Sisters of St. Joseph of Brentwood on the Feast of the Nativity of Mary, September 8.

Leaving her widowed mother and six siblings just two months after her father's death seemed out of the question, so Johnson told her mother that she would instead stay in Brooklyn and go to college there. But Margaret Johnson was adamant that her eldest daughter pursue her dream and calling. Beth remembers her mother telling her, "This is your life. Your father would want you to go forward with this." So she did.

In 1959 it wasn't unusual for a young woman to enter the convent, and few were surprised that Johnson chose religious life. She had always loved the beauty of the Catholic liturgy: the music, prayers, incense, flowers, and candles. Once she had reached fifth grade, she attended daily Mass, as required by the school, walking up the hill with her father for the 6:30 a.m. service, then back home for a bowl of oatmeal before school. Even during vacation and summers, young Beth still attended daily. Her sister Peggy remembers the blue alarm clock going off every morning at six. "To this day I know the song it would play," she says, noting that her sister's discipline "was so characteristic of her devotion to her faith, even at a very early age." Beth also loved Forty Hours Devotions, Stations of the Cross during Lent, and strewing rose petals in front of the monstrance.

The priests and sisters in the parish were kind, and the Redemptorist brother in charge of the annual Christmas pageant would treat the children to milk and cookies after practice. "They were good people, and good to us as kids," Johnson recalls. Her confessor instructed her to try to listen to God's call, but she couldn't initially hear God's voice clearly. She had already been told she couldn't be an airplane pilot or a tugboat driver—her first two career choices as a young child. Being denied those dreams because of her gender didn't bother her at the time. She just thought, "Well, that's just the way the world is. I'll do something else." When she was older, Johnson told a teacher that she wanted to be a Jesuit. "I can still hear her laughing," she says. "I was that naïve. To me, Jesuits did interesting things in the way of Christ—that was very attractive to me. When [the teacher] informed me I couldn't be a Jesuit because I wasn't a man, I thought, 'Oh well, a man can't be a sister of St. Joseph. I guess we each have our own ways.' "

Youthful questions aside, Johnson says she did not feel called to ordained priesthood, although she admits she might feel differently if she were starting out now. She is, however, passionately in favor of opening ordination to women. "It's terribly impoverishing for the whole church not having the ministry of women at that level," she says. A fellow feminist theologian once half joked that if the church had opened ordination to women in the 1970s, women would have been so busy caring for people as pastors that they wouldn't have had time to think about feminist theology. Instead, "it fell to me to be thinking about those things, rather than be busy in a parish caring for people," Johnson says.

By high school she wanted to become a teacher, like the sisters of St. Joseph she had had in grade school and high school, yet she didn't choose religious life just to teach. Instead, it was the prospect of a life devoted to the inner life that was most attractive to the teenage Beth. She remembers learning the "Magnificat" from her high school religion teacher, and the prayer got her thinking about how to build a relationship with God that was filled with goodness, love, and joy. As a religious woman, she could "have all that spiritual richness a part of your life every day and also be helping other people," she says. "Nothing else seemed as appealing as that. If you became a nun, you were giving your life to God. That really was the attraction."

She also had been surrounded by women religious in her family, with one nun on her mother's side of the family and five on her father's. "Our house was filled with nuns, as well as priests and bishops," recalls Peggy. "That was the culture we grew up in. The expected pathway for women was to be a nun or be a mother of seven children. Those were the choices we saw." Although she had done a lot of mothering of her siblings, Johnson never seriously considered marriage or motherhood, though there were certainly boys she liked while growing up. At that time, religious orders did not address issues of celibacy and sexuality very directly, but after Johnson made her vows and entered academia, she found herself surrounded by men, and "that whole aspect of life caught up with me." She admits she has fallen in love, but chose friendship instead. The call to religious life was too strong.

In later reflections, Johnson has repeatedly credited her religious congregation as a major influence and essential source of support throughout her life. Religious life "holds forth as an ideal an integrated life in which a person, rooted in faith, finds fulfillment in the giving of oneself in service to others," she wrote in a personal statement for a scholarship in the mid-1970s. "I find that as a member of this community I have a unique freedom to pursue my own quest for meaning and to integrate professional excellence with personal values. Living with other women who are also professionally competent and dedicated to a life of service continually enriches my own efforts in this regard."[1] Yet Johnson also recognized that her life as a scholar has meant a certain distance from community living. "I am not the type to sit around the TV with a beer nor around the teapot with endless talking," she admitted in a letter to her superior in 1980, "but I seek solitude on a daily basis to read and study and search."[2]

The order Johnson chose had its roots in seventeenth-century France. From its beginning, the Sisters of St. Joseph was a non-cloistered congregation that included women of all classes and backgrounds who initially supported themselves by making lace. Nearly destroyed during the French Revolution, the congregation was "refounded" by a sister who narrowly escaped the guillotine herself. The Sisters of St. Joseph became a teaching order and was eventually invited to Missouri in the 1830s to found a school for children who were deaf. A letter from the Countess Felicite de Duras in 1835 recommending that the sisters be sent to America described them as "ready for anything."[3]

That "can-do" spirit spread as the order grew in the United States, eventually prompting Bishop John Loughlin, the first bishop of Brooklyn, to invite St. Joseph sisters from Philadelphia to start a mission and school in New York. In 1903, the motherhouse and novitiate for that group were moved to Brentwood in Suffolk County, Long Island, which is where young Beth Johnson arrived in 1959. Today, the US Federation of Sisters of St. Joseph represents nearly five thousand sisters and three thousand associates in sixteen congregations. Their ministries include everything from education to social service, from activism to the arts—all inspired by "profound love of God and love of neighbor without distinction," according to their mission statement.[4] The Brentwood community sponsors Saint Joseph's College in New York as well as several high schools in New York and one in Puerto Rico. In the mid-twentieth century, St. Joseph sisters also staffed a number of elementary schools, including Our Lady of Perpetual Help, where young Beth Johnson was introduced to them. She remembers her religious women teachers as young, energetic, and fun—"people you'd like to spend time with."

Numbers in the Brentwood community are down from a high of more than two thousand sisters just before Vatican II to approximately six hundred today, but the order is financially strong, the result of both wise investing and, in part, the contributions from Johnson's best-selling books. Her vow of poverty means she owns nothing: her bank account and car are in the name of the Sisters of St. Joseph. "To tell you the honest truth, it's not a problem," Johnson says. "The least important thing to me is money." All her salary, royalties, and stipends for public lectures support the common good, in which she strongly believes. For example, one sister she was very close to was stricken with multiple sclerosis and became increasingly debilitated. "Here I am having this wonderfully exciting, spiritually satisfying life. It could have easily been me in that wheelchair," she says, noting that at least the money she earns helps pay that sister's medical bills.

Back in 1959, when her mother and siblings dropped her off at Brentwood, Johnson joined seventy-five other young women entering and preparing for religious life. She took the name Sr. Mary Walter, for her father. Yet her years in the novitiate, the period of formation and preparation before taking formal vows in a religious order, were not happy. She didn't mind the rigid schedule of getting up at 5:20 a.m. for morning prayers. In fact, she loved the silence and time for reflection—especially during the second year in which the novices were not allowed to study but only do physical work and receive spiritual instruction. But she struggled with the discipline around seemingly minor rule infractions. If a novice broke a rule—say, not making one's bed correctly—as penance she was required to kneel in the dining room with her arms extended and to request prayers from the other sisters as they came in to eat. "An awful lot of that I found kind of meaningless and not for the love of God," Johnson remembers.

Did she consider leaving? Not at the time, but Johnson later realized that if the Second Vatican Council had not happened, she most likely would not have remained. Certainly, in the years to come, many would leave religious life—more than 4,300 US nuns in the three-year span of 1963–66 alone.[5] "Shortly after Vatican II, people left in droves, and I wished them well," Johnson remembers. "But I still saw a lot of meaning in the way of life and still felt called. There was a sense of rightness to my life and what I was doing. I still had the goal of being good and loving and of having time for prayer. That was still very attractive to me." In a letter to her superior in 1980, Johnson admitted that a friend who was leaving the order talking excitedly about her own apartment "does not awaken any desire in me to do likewise but has the contrary effect."[6]

What got her through her novitiate years was focusing on her college studies at Brentwood College, the "Sister Formation College" founded in 1955 for novices and junior-professed Sisters of St. Joseph and those from other orders. (The college closed in the 1970s because of changes after Vatican II that allowed women religious to mingle with the "seculars" —meaning the rest of the baptized.) Johnson continued to excel academically. Her college average was a 93.75 percent, the first in her class of ninety-four students.[7] Her detractors today might be surprised to learn of straight As in two classes on dogma. But an economics course bored her. "The professor would go on and on about the rules of economics, and I was sitting in the back reading [Jesuit priest and poet] Gerard Manley Hopkins," she recalls.

Johnson and some friends created a "band of resistance," quietly rebelling against the rigidity of the novitiate. Karen Cavanaugh entered the Sisters of St. Joseph the same year as Johnson and had gone to her high school, although Cavanaugh had graduated a year earlier and worked before entering the convent. She compares the novitiate years to boot camp in the army or to the police academy. Again, it wasn't so much the rigidity of the schedule as the emphasis on renunciation and mortification that bothered the young postulants. "It was like you had to merit or earn God's love," Cavanaugh remembers. "So you would almost try to kill yourself so that God would forgive you and love you."

The young women found comfort in one another—and from some mentors in the older sisters. Cavanaugh and Johnson kept a black and white composition notebook called "Tangents," in which they wrote thoughts, prayers, and images from those who helped them think and pray "outside the box." Cavanaugh also remembers the faculty teaching some of the brightest postulants at night, with students moving from one portable chalkboard to another for extra instruction on history and theology. Johnson, of course, was among them. "She was an extremely bright young woman," recalls Cavanaugh, who went on to study theology herself and teach in secondary schools.

The emphasis on sacrifice in the novitiate was meant to foster humility—and perhaps was successful since nearly everyone describes Johnson as exceedingly humble despite her accomplishments. The Sisters of St. Joseph of Brentwood are proud of Johnson and her work, and they fully supported her during the controversy with the US bishops. When Johnson attended a congregation meeting during that time, hundreds of the sisters stood and applauded when she entered the room. Cavanaugh remembers being awed by Johnson's courage during the controversy, courage she suspects Johnson probably always had. As young women in the novitiate, Cavanaugh wasn't even aware that her friend had just lost her father. "You didn't know what everyone carried in that door when they entered the convent," she recalled. "You didn't know that people were carrying these kinds of pain."

Once a month, Johnson's mother and siblings would drive an hour each way on a Sunday for the two-hour visit with Beth at the motherhouse. Susan Johnson remembers the trips as both fun and somewhat "weird" to an outsider. Peggy remembers missing her older sister immensely. "We were so tight. We lived together in the same bedroom for fifteen years, and then suddenly she was gone and we weren't allowed to see her or touch her," Peggy says. "It must have been very hard on her, too, but I think that's a testimony to her faith and how strong it was."

Despite her assurances to her eldest daughter and the presentation of a brave face to the rest of the children, Margaret Johnson must have suffered terribly from the double whammy of losing her husband and first child that year. She began taking in foster babies to help put food on the table, Susan remembers. "We had dinner after dinner of pea soup, because that was all she could afford." Later, Margaret would use her college degree to teach high school math. Eventually, she took and passed the civil service exam in New York and began work as the administrator of the health insurance plan for the city's department of education. She never remarried, though she did date. The kids used to parody the television public service announcement on curfews, saying, "It's ten o'clock. Do you know where your mother is?"

"She kept putting one foot in front of the other," remembers Susan. "It was pretty remarkable. We all considered her pretty strong, both physically and spiritually." Beth also soldiered on, but in retrospect, she realizes that not attending to her grief most likely prolonged it. "In the pre-Vatican II novitiate there was absolutely no attention to one's emotional life," she says.

Johnson graduated from Brentwood College in 1964, one of nearly a hundred St. Joseph sisters to earn a bachelor of science degree in education that day. The order of exercises at commencement included the spiritual "Rock-a My Soul," an indication of the changing church.[8] Johnson's first teaching assignment was to fifth graders at a parish elementary school, where she found herself at loggerheads with her superior, who was also the school principal.

One day, while Johnson was practicing with the CCD students for the upcoming confirmation ceremony, during which the bishop would visit, the principal came to watch. She most likely wanted to know that the students would behave appropriately in front of the bishop and thus protect her reputation. Two towheaded kids from Johnson's class were misbehaving, so the principal grabbed them by the hair and banged their heads together. As the principal stormed out, she instructed Johnson to report to her office. Shocked by the use of physical violence, Johnson used the meeting to rebuke the principal. "How were you communicating the love of Jesus to them? You destroyed what we've been teaching them!" Johnson remembers saying.

The principal ordered her out of her office. In retrospect, Johnson laughs at her audacity. "Here I was, this young whippersnapper, telling this very senior person in this hierarchal system that she was wrong," she says. Yet, her gut and her passion demanded that she tell the truth. The next year she was transferred to another school and assigned to teach seventh- and eighth-grade science, math, and religion. Students remember her as a wonderful teacher, but Johnson's reputation as being difficult would continue with her next superior.

By then, *Perfectae Caritatis*, the Vatican II document on the renewal of religious life, had instructed religious to be open to the world, so the sisters' prayers included references to the Detroit race riots and the Vietnam War. Clergy and laity were joining the marches down Fifth Avenue with shouts of "Hey, hey, LBJ, how many kids did you kill today?" Johnson was told not to march in habit, but her conscience told her otherwise. She argued with her superior that the moral evils of racism and war negated her authority over her, comparing the situation to that of Germans and the Nazis. "A superior can order you to do anything except in matters that were sinful. I thought the war in Vietnam was sinful," Johnson says. "I told her, 'You do not have a right to tell me I cannot follow my conscience when it's a matter of life and death.'" The superior reported Johnson to the mother superior as "obstreperous and independent minded."

By the summer of 1965, John F. Kennedy had been assassinated, the Rev. Martin Luther King Jr. had marched on Washington, and President Lyndon B. Johnson had declared a War on Poverty. Johnson and her now-sixty classmates were on a two-month retreat at the motherhouse in preparation for final vows. Johnson was conflicted. The events of the Second Vatican Council in Rome were distant; without a television, the nuns had barely heard of it. "The trouble was that I was fascinated by this world," writes Johnson. "In contrast to what our vow preparation was teaching, I kept thinking that if God created and loved this world, then shouldn't those of us radically seeking God in religious life be in the forefront of engagement with this world?"[9]

One day, the retreatants were handed a copy of a poorly printed pamphlet, a draft of a conciliar document. Johnson took it on her daily walk, settled under the shade of a favorite pine tree, and began to read the opening words of *Gaudium et Spes* (the Pastoral Constitution on the Church in the Modern World): "The joys and the hopes, the griefs and the anxieties of the people of this age, especially those who are poor or in any way afflicted, these too are the joys and hopes, the griefs and the anxieties of the followers of Christ."[10] Johnson was riveted from those first words and spent the afternoon poring over the document. "Here was the highest authority in the church challenging the spiritual tradition in which I felt encased, endorsing rather than warning against involvement in the world," she writes. "The sun began to slide down the sky, but in a very real way the light was rising."[11]

On that hot, summer day, Johnson found the answer to her question. The pre-Vatican II church was where her faith took root, and she loved the sense of God's greatness and mystery, the beauty of the ritual, and the ethic of responsibility of care of neighbor that she had discovered in that church. That would not be repudiated or forgotten. But the Holy Spirit was blowing in the opened windows, hauling the Catholic Church into the modern age and urging it to engage with the world. This was a project to which Johnson could commit her life. She took her final vows and began her life as a religious woman in a church ready for reform.

CHAPTER THREE

Budding Scholar

Teaching and Learning after Vatican II

In December 1965, on the Feast of the Immaculate Conception, the Second Vatican Council officially came to a close with an address from Pope Paul VI, which contained "good news" for various groups of people who had looked to the council for inspiration. Cardinal Leon Duval of Algiers, Algeria, read the portion addressed to women: "The hour is coming, in fact has come, when the vocation of woman is being achieved in its fullness, the hour in which woman acquires in the world an influence, an effect and a power never hitherto achieved."[1]

Just four months earlier, Sr. Mary Walter Johnson had taken her final vows as a sister of St. Joseph of Brentwood and had begun her path as a scholar and theologian in service to that reforming church. Although she did not know it then, Johnson's vocation would include "an influence, an effect, and a power" not then expected from women in the church before Vatican II. In fact, it was the young nun's enthusiasm for the council that prompted her to abandon a previous plan to pursue a master's degree in science and instead ask her superiors if she could study theology.

When she first approached Mother Immaculata Maria with the idea, the superior wanted to know why Johnson wanted to study theology. Johnson told her it was because she had questions: How could God be three persons in one divine nature? And how could Christ be one person in two natures, human and divine? The elder nun said, "If I questioned like that, I would lose my faith." Johnson blurted out, "If I did *not* question like this, I would lose my faith." Mother Immaculata did not share Johnson's questioning, but she respected and would ultimately support her younger sister's yearning for greater understanding. In a scene right out of *The Sound of Music*, Mother Immaculata Maria said, "Go to Manhattan, my child, and find your faith."[2]

Every Saturday morning, Johnson would board the Long Island railroad train to Penn Station, where she transferred to the #1 subway and took it to the last stop. She had chosen Manhattan College, a Catholic school founded by De La Salle Christian Brothers in the Riverdale neighborhood of the Bronx, because by the late 1960s it already had a well-known program in post-Vatican II theology. In graduate school at Manhattan College, Johnson studied French Dominican Fr. Yves Congar, German Jesuit Fr. Karl Rahner ("who I didn't understand at that point," she says), and other theologians who had been advisors to the bishops at the council. Since reading Protestants was no longer forbidden, as it had been before Vatican II, she also read Protestant theologians for the first time: Karl Barth of the Reformed Church in Switzerland; Dietrich Bonhoeffer, the German Lutheran; and Jürgen Moltmann of the German Reformed Church. Johnson took to studying theology "like a fish to water," she says. "It was interesting and exciting and satisfying to my soul. . . . I was eager to learn."

Not surprisingly, she continued to be an excellent student, earning straight As and passing the French language requirement for her master's degree. After morning classes of Theological Anthropology, Judeo-Christian Morality, and Trends in Contemporary Protestantism, Johnson attended Mass at Manhattan College, where the priests were experimenting with new ways of worship and praying, including using the English vernacular, as *Sacrosanctum Concilium*, the Vatican II document on liturgy, now allowed. After a year of work toward her master's degree, the dean offered Johnson a new scholarship set up to assist women religious studying theology. It meant she could live on campus. The superiors from her religious order once again agreed, and Johnson moved in with thirteen other sisters from around the country. For the first time since she had entered the convent nine years earlier, she could take the subway to a museum, to the ticker tape parade on Broadway to celebrate astronauts Neil Armstrong and Buzz Aldrin, or to a Judy Collins concert. Grateful for the de-emphasis on obedience as the main virtue in religious life, she reveled in the freedom.

But it was what she was learning in the classroom that really excited Johnson, and she began writing papers that demonstrated a surprising degree of theological sophistication. The topics of some of her master's papers indicate her interests: "Pluralism and the Church," "Some Problems of Catechesis in a Secular Age," and "Freedom Today and the Book of Job." The latter was for her first course at Manhattan, Introduction to the Old Testament, in which the professor—Fr. Anthony Rubsys, from Lithuania via Rome after World War II—required the students to read the entire Hebrew Scriptures. The book of Job spoke not only to her personal suffering of the loss of her father, but to all the suffering in the world: poverty, war, violence, racism. "This wasn't abstract," she remembers. "The whole world was on fire, especially with the bombings and the war in Vietnam."

Johnson's brother was in the Air Force, but remained stationed in Guam and never saw battle, though many of his friends did. Johnson's paper on Job earned an A+ with the comment "Excellent" scrawled by the professor. However, in her archives, paper clipped to the essay is a rejection letter from *The Bible Today*, a journal published by Liturgical Press in Collegeville, Minnesota, noting that the decision to reject the paper for publication was painful because it was "interesting and challenging," but that the article was more "philosophical than biblical."[3]

The civil rights movement also was on Johnson's mind and heart, as two sisters from her congregation were with the Rev. Martin Luther King Jr. as he marched over the bridge in Selma, Alabama. Johnson did not make that trip but did join protests against the Vietnam War in New York and worked on the presidential campaign of Senator Eugene McCarthy, whose antiwar platform challenged incumbent Lyndon Johnson. "There was a sense of power in having had a hand (admittedly small) in the unseating of a president, but also a sense of having been betrayed in the trust I had put in government (my first presidential ballot had been cast for Johnson),"[4] Johnson wrote in a later personal statement for a Danforth Foundation scholarship. The controversy around Pope Paul VI's encyclical on birth control, *Humanae Vitae*, in 1968, also rattled Johnson and created something of a personal crisis, causing her "to radically question the ultimate nature of any authority, and to search deeper for the sources of truth."[5] And the assassinations of the Rev. Martin Luther King Jr. and Robert Kennedy "shook me profoundly and led me to question the worth of goodness and service to others and even of life itself."[6]

Yet Johnson saw her theological studies as her way to contribute to these wider societal issues. In the summer of

1969, Johnson took her comprehensive exams. One question asked her to analyze the "dialectic between exclusive and inclusive, structured and nonstructured descriptions of the Christian church . . . and how ecclesiology since Vatican II has overcome certain historical exaggerations in one direction or the other . . . [as well as] implications that these developments have for the ecumenical movement and the challenge to the credibility of the contemporary church."[7] Johnson does not remember her particular response to that question, but she does recall how significantly inclusive the change in the church's position toward non-Catholics was.

"When I was growing up, I wasn't allowed to even go into a Protestant church," she says. The Vatican II document *Nostra Aetate* (the Declaration on the Relation of the Church with Non-Christian Religions) called other Christians "brethren" instead of "heretics" and actually said that God's grace extended to them. "To see what had been portrayed all my childhood as the enemy take on the contour as the ally and the friend—it was mind-blowing," says Johnson, who would later go on to serve on the National Lutheran/Catholic Dialogue in the 1980s and '90s.

She passed her written comps and by February of 1970 had completed all the work for her master's degree in religious studies. By the time she graduated, she did so as Sr. Elizabeth Johnson, having returned to her baptismal name after her congregation had voted on such reforms as part of renewals of religious life required by Vatican II. Like many other communities of religious women, the Sisters of St. Joseph had also voted to accept a modified habit in lieu of the traditional garb in the late 1960s. Johnson switched "as soon as I could," she recalls.

For years she had worn the habit of black wool, which covered her entire body, except for her face and hands. It wasn't so much the physical discomfort—although the habit was not comfortable—but the message the dress sent that bothered Johnson. "As a young American woman in the '60s, I didn't think it expressed the spirituality I felt called to," she says. "It set you apart and put you on a pedestal, making you seem more perfect than other people. None of that made any sense to me." When the Sisters of St. Joseph researched the history of their order as part of post-Vatican II reforms, they discovered that the young women who founded the community were peasants who had worn the dress of the day so they could connect with people rather than be set apart. Once Johnson was able to wear regular street clothes, she reveled in the luxury of possible anonymity on the subway.

With her master's degree completed, Johnson was assigned to the Academy of St. Joseph on the grounds of the motherhouse in Brentwood, where she would teach high school religion to young women, many of whom she keeps in contact with today. But the transition from the intellectualism of graduate school to the petty problems of fourteen-year-olds was not an easy one for Johnson. In a mimeographed letter to her friends from Manhattan College, she wrote that the school was "not as awful as anticipated, but still pretty bad."[8] Johnson lived in the dorms with the residential students, whose blasting radios and loud voices were psychologically draining. Down the hall were a group of two sophomores and five freshmen; they included the daughter of the vice president of Haiti, a young woman from Venezuela, a girl who had lost both parents, the daughter of a multilingual translator from the Dominican Republic, and the daughter of a policewoman.[9] Needless to say, Johnson had her hands full.

Just as the church was changing in the late 1960s and early '70s, so was education, and the faculty at the Academy of St. Joseph was experimenting with innovative teaching methods that focused on the student rather than exclusively on the subject matter. Johnson remembers the changes as coming from a "vision and spirituality of corporate friend-ship and community" among the faculty and administration. She enthusiastically embraced this pedagogical shift, using contemporary films and music in her classes, and once hav-ing students cut out paper dolls to prompt a discussion on conformity.

For most of her students, Johnson was the first person to show them how to apply the historical-critical method to the Scriptures and to point out that the Bible should not always be taken literally. One student wrote in a letter to Johnson: "I liked [this course] because it made you think and question." Another said she often found the Bible hard to understand, but that Johnson's course seemed to "open my eyes . . . I was so convinced that there was an Adam and Eve and apple, and now wow! It's a myth to explain a happening." That student also admitted that for the first time she found herself excited to explore the Scriptures.[10] Johnson's evaluations indicated her teaching was "excellent," and one noted that "S. Beth is giving our students a very scholarly approach to religion today."[11] Toward the end of her tenure, the students gave her "The Caring Award" for her teaching and mentorship. De-spite the challenges at the beginning, Johnson remembers her eight years at St. Joseph (1969–77) as "a wonderful moment in my life," a time of growth and a chance to put her prin-ciples and ideals into action.

During those years, Johnson also worked in parishes, became an extraordinary minister of Communion, and began speaking to groups in the area. In a run-off election, Johnson was elected to be on the sisters advisory board to the bishop. "Would you believe!!!!" she wrote at the time.

"I'm elated at the vote of confidence, but scared at the encounter, which may turn into confrontation."[12] That letter to friends also relates the story of a car accident. One evening, several sisters were driving to Manhattan to hear Catholic author Eugene Kennedy speak on "Sex in the Church," when their car went over a wall and down a cliff. One of the sisters yelled, "Jesus!"—"a traditionalist through and through," Johnson wrote. "I called out twice, 'Let's get the hell out of this car'—the secular man [sic] through and through."[13] Luckily, no one was hurt, though they did not get to hear the lecture.

She also began teaching college courses at St. Joseph's College, which led to her consideration for doctoral studies by her order. The college was expanding, and the order needed more faculty, so they were sending their members to work on doctoral degrees in various fields. Johnson remembers Sr. Joan de Lourdes, the superior at the time, musing that the church was going to need women theologians. Johnson looked into and applied to a number of schools; her superior wanted Johnson to study at the Pontifical Gregorian University in Rome, but allowed Johnson to make her own choice. Johnson decided against the all-male environment of Rome. The feminist movement was underway and interested her. "My instinct just was that [Rome] was not the place for me," she says. "I wanted an American degree, where women could have some say."

Johnson had been accepted and offered full-ride scholarships in the doctoral programs at Yale Divinity School, the University of Notre Dame, Boston College, and others. To decide which school to attend, she sat down with the academic catalogs for each to compare the course offerings and faculty. She was impressed with the Catholic University of America in Washington, DC, which in her opinion had the strongest program in systematic theology. The faculty was top-notch, including Jesuit Fr. Avery Dulles on theology, Jesuit Fr. Joseph Fitzmyer on biblical studies, and Fr. Charles Curran on moral theology.

In the "statement of purpose" in her application to CUA in the spring of 1977, Johnson wrote that she wanted to study systematic theology and make a contribution toward contemporary understanding of theological issues. "In a very real sense I feel that I have reached the limits of my knowledge, and, since I am basically a thinking, seeking person, the need for further systematic study becomes obvious," she wrote. "Furthermore, I have a desire to make a contribution myself in the field of systematic theology, dialoguing with our ancient tradition from the standpoint of the American experience, of the American woman's experience. There is a dearth of good women theologians in our Church, in all the churches, and I would expect that in some way I could make an enriching contribution."[14]

Johnson's religious community fully supported her in her graduate work in theology. A letter confirming her assignment to full-time doctoral studies at CUA pointed out that the Sisters of St. Joseph's constitution stated that a sister's mission "is to reveal God's love and to facilitate the *healing*, life-giving effects of that discovery. Her ministry is *any* activity or presence through which this mission is realized."[15] She also felt supported by the leadership at Catholic University. The dean of the school of theology, Fr. Carl J. Peter, became a mentor and was very supportive of women religious pursuing graduate theological studies. When he called to offer the scholarship, Johnson told him about her offers from other schools and bluntly asked about academic freedom. She also remembers how Peter ended the conversation: "He said, 'I certainly hope you will come to Catholic University, but it is your decision, Sister, because if you come and you are unhappy, I do not want to be responsible for your misery.' "

Johnson was not miserable; in fact, she remembers her years at CUA as a doctoral student as "golden years," in terms of the quality of both the intellectual stimulation and friendships. But she had no women professors and read no books written by women for her classes. While there were women in the religious education department, Johnson and two other religious women were the first to pursue doctoral studies in theology at CUA. "We were women moving into a field where there were no women ahead of us," Johnson says. "We weren't angry, and we didn't make a big deal out of it, but there was a sense among us that we were doing something new."

Sister Mary Catherine Hilkert, OP, vividly remembers the first time she met Johnson. It was the fall of 1977 and both were new students at Catholic University. Hilkert was starting her master's, and Johnson was beginning her doctoral studies. Regan Hall had been designated as the separate "nuns' dorm," and both were moving in. As Hilkert arrived, she remembers seeing Johnson down the hall, dressed in cutoffs, a red T-shirt, and a neck brace (from a minor summer boating accident), painting the ceiling of her room. "I think she even brought the paint with her," says Hilkert. "She always thinks ahead like that. Here it was a hot and humid August, and we were all under a lot of stress. But for her, the way to move in was to have everything spic and span."

Johnson was known as extremely studious and someone who never did anything halfway. "She was always the first one up in that dorm, or at least on my floor," Hilkert remembers. "When you walked by her room, the sun would be shining, she would already have her tea and be sitting at her desk, preparing for the Greek exam—which she took at the first possible date to get it out of the way, and of course passed with flying colors. This was all before any of us got to the dining hall for breakfast."

An introvert, Johnson nonetheless values friendships and cultivated many at Catholic University that would become lifelong ones. She was the one who would suggest an outing to the Kennedy Center or to see the Matisse cutouts at the National Gallery. As graduate students, the women were counting their pennies, and Johnson was especially frugal. Once, after a performance of Handel's "Messiah" at the Kennedy Center, other concertgoers were enjoying champagne in the lobby. Beth opened up her purse, pulled out two plastic cups, and a little wine and scotch she had brought along. Another example of their thriftiness is that after Johnson passed her doctoral exams a friend hung a multipaneled "Congratulations" card on her door. The group continues to pass the card around whenever any of them has an honor. "And that card has been in the same faded, purple file folder for thirty-eight years," Hilkert says.

The female students from both the theology and the religious education departments at CUA formed a somewhat clandestine women's discussion group, complete with T-shirts emblazoned with the acronym WIT, for the club name Women in Theology. The group read the earliest Christian feminist theologians' work "under the cover of darkness, like Nicodemus going to Jesus at night," Johnson recalls. They knew how lucky they were to be studying theology at all, since earlier generations of women had literally sat in the hallways just to hear theological lectures. Today WIT lives on as a blog (womenintheology.org) written by younger, primarily Catholic feminist theologians but acknowledges its feminist foremothers for whom it is named.

But Hilkert would not have called Johnson a feminist during those early years. For example, although some students were using inclusive language when writing papers, in some of Johnson's early papers she still used "men" in a generic way to refer to both men and women. The WIT group invited women like Sr. Sandra Schneiders and Elisabeth Schüssler Fiorenza (whose husband, Francis, was teaching at CUA at the time) to speak. "We had no female faculty and no real encouragement to study serious works by women, including doctors of the church," Hilkert remembers.

Although all the students at Catholic University were bright, Johnson stood out even then, Hilkert remembers. "She really was extraordinary and had the keenest mind," she says. Johnson was a few years older than the other students and had already taught at the college level. She also had already studied Aquinas's *Summa Theologica*, the classic, encyclopedia-length work on Catholic theology. Although the program was not cutthroat, nor were the women in competition, Johnson was seen as excelling above the others. "She did not only all the required reading, but also all the recommended reading," Hilkert remembers.

One day, Johnson went to talk to a mentor of hers on the faculty about the stress of graduate school. He asked her to tell him about her typical day. She described how she got up early, studied Greek, went to classes, studied some more, attended the noon liturgy at Caldwell Hall, had lunch, studied some more. "Finally, by five in the afternoon, a group of us get together . . ." she said. Her mentor interrupted, "Oh, good!" But then she finished, ". . . to pray." His advice: "I'll tell you what's wrong with your life—unrelieved religion!"

Johnson took the advice to heart, but the intellectual and theological education was exhilarating to her. She took a course on Karl Rahner and "finally understood what he was

about," she remembers. That first Christmas, she photo-
copied a twenty-five-page paper she had written about
Rahner and grace, rolled the copies, and tied them with a
red ribbon as gifts for her friends and family. "My mother
thought I was absolutely nuts, but I just wanted everyone
to understand how gracious God was toward us," Johnson
remembers.

As Johnson was beginning the second year of her doctoral
program, Pope Paul VI died. Then after the thirty-three-day
papacy of Pope John Paul I, the cardinals elected the church's
first Polish pope, a young man named Karol Józef Wojtyła
who would take the name John Paul II. As the white smoke
emerged from the Sistine Chapel in Rome, bells rang across
the campus of CUA. "Everybody was thrilled; it was so
exciting," Johnson remembers. No one—including Johnson
—had any idea how much this new pope would change the
direction of the church and her own life.

CHAPTER FOUR

Awakened Feminist

Finding Her Voice at CUA

Pope John Paul II had already visited Boston, New York City, Philadelphia, Des Moines, and Chicago before concluding his weeklong, whirlwind first visit to the United States in the nation's capital, where he met with President Jimmy Carter in the Oval Office—the first pope ever to visit the White House. The next day, October 7, 1979, the pope came to the Catholic University of America, where he was scheduled to give an academic address. On the way to that event in the CUA gymnasium, John Paul II was scheduled to stop and give a blessing to religious women gathered at the Basilica of the National Shrine of the Immaculate Conception.

They were ready for him. Discouraged by remarks made earlier in his trip that indicated the pope was closed to the prospect of opening ordination to women, activists from the recently formed Women's Ordination Conference and Washington-based Catholics for Equality had kept vigil outside the basilica all night. (The women's ordination movement had gotten a boost two years earlier when the Episcopal Church in the United States began ordaining women to the priesthood.) By morning, some three thousand women religious had arrived for the historic meeting. Beth Johnson was one of them.

Johnson and her CUA classmates arrived at 6:00 a.m., going through security with the Secret Service while it was still dark. The activists handed out blue armbands, representing Mary and the cause of women in the church. Johnson put hers in her pocket. While they waited for the pope to arrive, the women sang hymns and received condescending instructions from the Secret Service. "They spoke to us like we were in the first grade," including a warning not to do anything "untoward," Johnson remembers. The scoldings prompted some to put on their armbands. Johnson's remained in her pocket.

As John Paul II processed into the basilica, the crowd cheered. Johnson had a good seat, just a few seats in from the aisle and about a quarter of the way back from the altar. Next, Sr. Theresa Kane, RSM, president of LCWR, approached the podium to offer words of greeting. Johnson had heard rumors Kane might challenge the pope. About halfway through Kane's brief welcome, Sr. Mary Mahar, SSND, a CUA classmate, grabbed Johnson's arm and whispered, "She's going to say it."

Kane's words would become historic: She asked the pope to be "mindful of the intense suffering and pain which is part of the life of many women in these United States" and to "listen with compassion and to hear the call of women who comprise half of humankind." Not referencing the ordination issue directly, she said that the church "in its struggle to be faithful to its call for reverence and dignity for all persons must respond by providing the possibility of women as persons being included in all ministries of our Church." She concluded, "I urge you, Your Holiness, to be open to and respond to the voices coming from the women of this country who are desirous of serving in and through the Church as fully participating members."[1]

There were gasps from those in the audience, and Kane was interrupted many times by applause. When Kane finished, Johnson was on her feet cheering as part of a thundering, ten-minute response, clapping not only for Kane but for all women in the church. And she finally put on her blue armband. Johnson calls it "the day I became a feminist in the church."

In Johnson's papers at the University of Notre Dame archives, an entire folder is dedicated to October 7, 1979. In the folder are her ticket to the papal event, a piece of the blue armband, a copy of a letter to her superior, and a letter to her mother, on which is stapled a piece of the red carpet the pope walked on. In the letter to Sr. John Raymond McGann, Johnson sums up the day: "I saw the Pope, I prayed with the Pope, I applauded the Pope, and I didn't applaud the Pope; and each to me was extremely significant."[2] She was particularly discouraged by the pope's address, which she wrote, "could have been written in the 19th century, I think, with hardly a change. . . . I was disappointed in it, more for what he didn't say than for what he did. . . . I did not feel affirmed in my life as a woman religious in America."[3] However, she did note that the only times when the more traditional, habited nuns and the more progressive ones in blue armbands in the audience both applauded were at the pope's mention of the necessity of prayer and when he said, "Praised be Jesus Christ."[4]

Her reaction to Kane, in her letters and after some reflection, was more ambiguous. Johnson admired the fellow New Yorker's courage but wondered if she should have spoken so frankly. She was encouraged by her professor, Jesuit Fr. Avery Dulles, who told her it was "a great symbol of the

dynamic at work in the Church: the hierarchical office taking a position; the prophetic office raising a voice of challenge; and both in communion (the blessing given and
received),"[5] she wrote to her superior. In reporting Kane's
words, Johnson underlined the word *listen* in her sentence
about the desire of many women for full ministry within
the church. "My one thought as I applauded was that, regardless of ordination, I was expressing to John Paul II that
women, at least in America, have come of age, that we have
more to give than is usually realized, that we *are*."[6] In the
letter to her mother, she further pondered the meaning of
the day: "The future raises in us both hope and anxiety; it
comes to us from the side of the unknown, and its uncertainty both draws and repels. But we go on into this unknown future—our hope is stronger than anxiety—because
God is faithful to his promise and will be there."[7]

For her bravery, Kane would receive death threats and be
vilified by traditionalist Catholics who opposed opening
ordination to women and who saw Kane's words as disre-
spectful. But for Johnson and a generation of women religious, it was a significant, life-changing event. Twenty-five
years later, at a celebration of Kane's fiftieth year of religious
life, a small group of friends began reminiscing about the
significance of that October day in Washington, about how
it changed the church and how the church does theology.
More personally, it had transformed them as individuals;
significantly, they all still had their blue armbands. As
Johnson says, "My eyes were opened, and once you see
something, you can't unsee it." Surely this encounter of
solidarity with fellow women in the face of the church hierarchy would inform and inspire Johnson's later work.

However, first Johnson had to finish graduate school and
her doctoral dissertation. Her new feminist consciousness

may have made her questions more pressing, but it did not show up overtly in her work, at least initially. Just three months after the pope's visit, Johnson completed her comprehensive exams, which included a question on the use of the term "sinful church," especially by theologians Karl Rahner and Hans Küng. All three faculty on her comps board agreed that she passed with distinction, including Avery Dulles, who later wrote in a recommendation, "I can say that Sr. Elizabeth is one of the most able and promising students we have in our department. . . . Modest in proposing her views, she nevertheless has balanced and creative insights to offer."[8] After turning in her written comps, which she described in a note as "not works of art but done under pressure," she went to the movies.[9]

Johnson's doctoral dissertation was about German Lutheran theologian Wolfhart Pannenberg, who had studied under Karl Barth. Titled, "Analogy, Doxology, and Their Connection with Christology in the Theology of Wolfhart Pannenberg," the dissertation is cited in numerous scholarly books and other publications. Notably, she did not write explicitly about women in the church. The topic was her choice; she was interested in Christology and intrigued by Pannenberg's reflections on the centrality of Christ's resurrection. Her dissertation connected his work with theories of religious language and what words about God really mean—a topic she would return to in *She Who Is*. While working on her dissertation, she kept a copy of her typed drafts in a pillowcase near her window so she could throw them to safety in case of a fire. A second copy was entrusted to her Aunt Barbara's safe on Wall Street.[10] As a graduation present, her aunt gave her niece a trip to Europe and accompanied her on the trip, during which Johnson gave Pannenberg a copy of her dissertation. She also brought an invitation for the

Protestant scholar to speak at Catholic University, which at that time would have been seen as a feather in CUA's cap. He accepted and spoke there that next fall.

When Johnson received her doctorate in theology in 1981, she and Mary Ann Fatula, OP, did so as the first women to graduate from CUA with that degree. Johnson graduated with a 4.0 grade point average and had passed all three written and oral comps with distinctions. Her dissertation proposal had gone through on the first draft, a rare accomplishment. At the graduation ceremonies, Johnson wore an academic robe bequeathed to her by the Sisters of St. Joseph superior who had encouraged and approved her studies at CUA, Sr. Joan de Lourdes. She still wears that robe to this day.[11] The dean of the school of theology, Fr. Carl J. Peter, wrote of Johnson that "In sixteen years of teaching I have never taught a more intellectually gifted student. . . . She is at the very top of our student body of over 520 graduate students. She will be a systematician who will leave a mark on American theology."[12]

In fact, the theology department at CUA was so impressed with Johnson that they recruited her to join the faculty after she completed her doctorate. As a student, she had already been asked to step in to teach a Christology course at CUA after the priest assigned to the class had to leave midsemester to care for his ill parents. Because she had experience teaching college students and seminarians from her time in New York, the department chair asked Johnson to fill in. She was tempted to decline, instead needing to focus on finishing her dissertation, but she missed teaching. Her superior agreed it would be a good idea "to get her toe in the water." Johnson revamped the entire syllabus to bring in new ideas, which thrilled the students, who included seminarians not only from CUA but from other Catholic and Protestant theological schools that were part of a consortium to which CUA also belonged. Johnson was asked to teach the course again in the spring, and forty-nine students showed up on the first day, most of them from consortium schools.

It was in the middle of that course that CUA offered her a full-time, tenure-track position. It is unusual for a university to hire one of its own newly minted doctoral students, and Catholic University was looking for a feminist, or at least a woman theologian to diversify the faculty. Johnson had not shown much public interest in feminist theology, yet she was such a bright scholar and capable teacher that there was no opposition to her hiring from the faculty, remembers Fr. Charles Curran, who taught moral theology. At the time, out of a faculty of fifty-five, there were only two women—one in religious education, the other in liturgy. Johnson would be the first tenure-track woman to teach theology at the school.

Once again, Johnson found herself discerning a fork in her life's path. The choice was between returning to Brentwood to teach at the Sisters of St. Joseph's college or to accept the position at CUA. The former was a teaching college and was familiar; the latter had the pressure of research, tenure, and becoming a functioning scholar, including writing. "I was feeling very pulled toward the scholarly life, but it was scary," Johnson remembers. To discern this difficult decision, Johnson's superior sent her on an eight-day retreat in Pennsylvania, where she spent time in prayer and sat on a hillside writing out a list of pros and cons. She later wrote she hadn't given "any decision so much thought and prayer since I struggled through the decision to enter [religious life]."[13]

On the one hand, she was drawn to the offer and saw it as "a call to be stretched, to be more, to be involved in the work of the Church in a surprising new way."[14] The position would also clearly give her, as a woman, a chance to influence the future priests and bishops who would study at CUA. "It is not the abrasive women who will make inroads but the competent ones," she wrote Sr. John Raymond McGann, "and I could prepare the way now for the next generation of women to gain a better place in the Church."[15] On the other hand, it was unusual for a sister from their community to live away from Brentwood indefinitely, and as a "homebody at heart," Johnson longed to return to her community and to "most of the people I love in the world" in New York.[16] She also recognized that CUA would be "grueling, a 'publish or perish' situation, with all kinds of demands."[17] Yet, she did see the opportunity for a "vocation (to be a scholar) within a vocation (being a woman religious)"[18] as consistent with the community's constitution and her own vocation. "My choice of theology all along as a major and the unforced zest with which I have studied and taught it show that this is really my way to God," she wrote.[19]

When she returned to the motherhouse still unsure what to do, Sr. John Raymond came to a pragmatic decision: Johnson would go to Catholic University, but if it didn't work out, she could always return to New York to teach. "In the end, [McGann] said, 'We will mission you to CU and we'll give you as a gift to the wider church,'" Johnson recalls. "This was very typical of women's religious orders. The leaders had an ear to the Spirit." That decision to join the full-time faculty at CUA in 1981, of course, changed the rest of her life.

Although Johnson was used to all-male environments, she felt a heavy burden to succeed at CUA and later identified with astronaut Sally Ride, the first woman in space. She remembers her male coworkers as supportive and collegial colleagues. Her students were primarily seminarians from the fifty-six Catholic dioceses that sent students to the university, although the school was attracting an increasing number of lay people, including women, especially to the doctoral program. When she was hired, Johnson had never written anything for publication; the one article she had submitted (the paper on Job) had been rejected. She had to find her public voice and have that voice recognized by other scholars so she could get tenure. She was plagued by fears and recalls worrying: "Can I publish academically reputable ideas in academically reputable places that other scholars find worthy? Can I publicly join a conversation that has been going on for two thousand years in the church but has been conducted mainly by ordained men, except for an occasional mystic?"

She was tempted to join the boys' club and not rock the boat, but her conscience wouldn't allow her to play it so safe. "Something in me wouldn't let me," she remembers, instead feeling compelled to share how she saw things differently as a woman. She would bring up women's issues at department meetings. "That made people nervous, but something in me couldn't keep quiet," she says.

Yet Johnson's vocation was not to activism, but rather to theological thinking and writing. Now a decade and a half after the end of the Second Vatican Council, it was becoming clear that the insights of prophetic theologians who had been condemned before the council were now being accepted as truth. Johnson came to believe that "if you're a theologian worth your salt, that's what you do. You stay true to what your mind and heart think, especially if you're looking at the church and saying it needs to change." She realized she had to bring up justice issues about women in the church, but she would use the tradition itself to call the church to reform.

Johnson was no flaming radical. In fact, in one of her first published articles, she criticized feminists who were dismissing Mary because of the church's emphasis on her obedience, passivity, virginity, and role as a mother. Although she agreed with those feminist critiques of traditional teaching on Mary, Johnson challenged the dismissal of such an important part of Catholic tradition. Drawing on Scripture and Pope Paul VI's 1974 apostolic letter on Mary (*Marialis Cultus*, "For the Right Ordering and Development of Devotion to the Blessed Virgin Mary"), Johnson's article urged the church to change the hymns, prayers, and religious imagination around Mary to support women's equality and full humanity.[20] (She would later expand on this thesis in her 2003 book *Truly Our Sister*, which would be hailed as both feminist and grounded in church tradition.) The article, "The Marian Tradition and the Reality of Women," published in 1985 in *Horizons*, the journal of the College Theological Society, would not be so well received by members of the church hierarchy. In fact, it became the center of an effort to discredit Johnson and deny her tenure at CUA.

During the 1986–87 school year, all of Johnson's fears about succeeding as a woman in academia came true. In the fall of 1986, she applied for tenure, which the tenure committee, faculty senate, and president unanimously approved in early spring. Among those writing letters of support was a seminarian from the Philippines, Luis Antonio G. Tagle, who called her "a woman of faith and learning, of profound knowledge of the biblical and ecclesial roots of belief in Jesus, of sensitivity to the contemporary state of theology, of apostolic solicitude for God's beloved poor and oppressed."[21] Colleague Fr. David Power, OMI, in his review of Johnson, wrote that she had "a deep respect for the great Tradition" and a "natural orthodoxy, of the kind that becomes a theologian: the intellectual kind." His only criticism was that she could "afford to give herself some more free reign to be a bit more adventuresome and even more passionate."[22]

The recommendation for tenure was forwarded to the university's board for approval, usually a pro forma step. However, because of CUA's status as a pontifical university, the university's board of trustees includes the six cardinals in the United States. Perhaps because of her status as the first woman up for tenure in theology at CUA, the board, chaired by Cardinal James Hickey of Washington, had forwarded her dossier to Rome, where the CDF in Rome flagged the article on Mary. Curiously, also serving on the CUA board of trustees at that time was Johnson's former superior, Sr. Joan de Lourdes, by that point a canon lawyer who Johnson says "mounted a vigorous defense on my behalf."[23]

Her tenure application was put on hold, and Johnson began the harrowing process of responding to the cardinals' concerns that summer. She even received a pink slip from the university. Johnson was terrified. She couldn't eat or sleep. Her then superior, Sr. Clara Santoro, told her the one thing she needed to get through it was . . . a kitten! Johnson drove to New York to pick up the cat her superior had picked out for her. Johnson named her Shifra, after one of the Hebrew midwives in Exodus who defied the pharaoh and saved the male babies he had ordered killed. Johnson received support from others in her community as well. Her former superior, Sr. John Raymond, wrote a letter of encouragement, which Johnson keeps in her Bible to this day. "Don't do this if it kills you. But try to find joy in the cross of criticism," she wrote. "Don't strive to be so orthodox and safe that you sell short the ministry of the theologian and lose your way. The real victory is your integrity." In a postscript, she added, "Put more money in your budget for recreation."[24]

The first step in responding to the cardinals involved answering a series of written questions (called the *dubia*, or "doubts," in Latin). The question topics were wide-ranging, from her writings on Mary, feminism, and images of God, to "the role of a teacher of Catholic theology."[25] Johnson sought and received help from her CUA colleagues, including Jesuit Fr. Ladislas Orsy, professor of canon law; Fr. Joseph Komonchak, professor of ecclesiology in the Department of Religion and Religious Education, and Fr. Power, to assist her with what would become a forty-page, detailed, and careful response to the *dubia*. One example: for a question about Canon 752 that says theologians must give *obsequium religiosum* of mind and will to the magisterium, what is now known as a *mandatum*, Orsy, who had studied how the word *obsequium* had been translated in some twenty languages, helped craft a response that sidestepped any controversy by noting that canon lawyers of the world couldn't even settle on its meaning.

Johnson was not the only scholar facing investigation by the hierarchy; her colleague Fr. Charles Curran's troubles had been perhaps the most public. Curran, a priest of the Diocese of Rochester, New York, had joined the faculty at CUA as professor of Christian ethics in 1965. Two years later, he tussled with the university's administration over his dissenting views about the prohibition against artificial birth control, but after protests by students and faculty, was reinstated with tenure. His public opposition to *Humanae Vitae*, Pope Pius VI's 1968 encyclical reaffirming church teaching about contraception, and other questioning of some Catholic moral teachings on sexuality kept him on the Vatican's radar. In the 1980s, Curran was once again under investigation by the CDF, culminating in a meeting with then Cardinal Joseph Ratzinger in Rome. In 1986, the Vatican declared him "unsuitable" to teach Catholic theology.

Curran remembers Johnson as a "staunch supporter" during his troubles, and today the two are close friends. Some think their controversies were linked, that Johnson got caught up in the Vatican's pushback against CUA. During the 1985 investigation of Curran, Johnson and Dulles drafted a letter to the pope on behalf of Curran, testifying to his excellence in teaching and integrity as a scholar and a priest. The majority of the faculty signed it, but Johnson's department chair cautioned her to think twice about the move, since it could have negative ramifications for her in the future. She thought, "We were just telling the truth. If a theologian can't speak honestly to the pope, without being penalized, why be a theologian?" But she took her chair's words to heart, went home and stayed up all night with her Bible and a lit candle, and prayed about what to do. In the end, she signed it. "They radicalized me," Johnson says now. "They pushed me to wake up and take a stand. It was either that or tuck your tail between your legs and not have integrity."

She was determined to keep her integrity in her own tenure battle, as well. The next step was an in-person interrogation with cardinals Bernardin of Chicago, Law of Boston, and Hickey of Washington, representing the CDF in late September of 1987. One day, in the weeks before the meeting, Johnson received a message to call Cardinal Bernardin at his private number at the Chicago seminary in Mundelein, Illinois. Bernardin's personal theologian had read Johnson's Mary article and found nothing doctrinally objectionable, so he suspected the CDF's concerns were not correct or fair, Johnson says. "So we had several conversations leading up to this oral interrogation, you could call them 'coaching sessions.' He would say, 'If so-and-so asks a question in this way, this is what he's listening for,'" Johnson says. While the cardinal initially swore Johnson to secrecy about the calls, he later released her from that promise when he was dying.[26]

The interrogation, held at the University Club in Washington, DC, was a formal, legal process, and Johnson had to retain legal counsel. She also insisted that a court reporter transcribe the proceedings, which all participants signed as agreement of what had transpired, to prevent any temptation to stretch or misrepresent Johnson's words. Fathers Joseph Komonchak and David Power attended as her advisors. The day before, Johnson hiked around the arboretum and decided to face her fears about the impending interrogation in union with those detained unjustly in South Africa, where she had traveled in 1987. That morning, dressed in a red, white, and blue blouse as a symbol of "revolution against tyrants,"[27] she drove to the University Club, running red and yellow lights out of nervousness. Power would later say that while she went through red lights *on the way* to the meeting, she "stopped at all the red ones *during*—even the yellows."[28]

She refused to play the helpless female during the interrogation, nor was she co-opted into being collegial when Cardinal Hickey joked during small talk beforehand that he wondered what it would have been like for him, thirty years ago, to have had to appear at 8:00 a.m. to defend his theology to "a curmudgeon of an archbishop."[29] She prayed to Holy Wisdom for guidance, and for the most part, stuck to her strategy of not answering beyond what was asked, talking around controversial questions, and analyzing every word she spoke so as not to add fuel to the fire.

It was difficult, because Cardinal Law of Boston was "hostile" during the proceedings, Johnson remembers. In his questions, Law excerpted parts of the article where Johnson was quoting other scholars, then attributed those thoughts to her. For example, Law accused her of saying

Mary was not a model for women because she's a mother—when Johnson's article was actually criticizing that view, Johnson recalls. Another question from Law involved whether Mary was "higher" than other saints in heaven. Given her recent involvement with Lutheran-Catholic dialogue, Johnson was reluctant to undermine that ecumenical work, so her answer rambled about general theology of saints and diverted from the question. When Law tried to question her on women's ordination, she was saved by Bernardin, who noted that she had not written on that topic.[30]

As she looked out at the three cardinals and their theological advisers, all wearing black and facing Johnson, who was literally on trial for her career, she had this image of immature eighth-grade boys right before graduation—which all good teachers know they cannot fight by declaring war against them. Instead, you have to divert their negative energy into something productive. When Law twisted her words, she thought, "You're not going to get my goat."

As Cardinal Law paged through the three-ring binder containing all of Johnson's writings, Cardinal Bernardin moved the group to make a decision, suggesting each cardinal share his thoughts so far. "I'll go first," he said, and proceeded to say favorable things about Johnson and her work. Cardinal Hickey was smiling during his comments, so Johnson assumed he was also won over. Cardinal Law slammed the binder shut and acquiesced, mentioning that since she mostly wrote in the area of Christology, she wouldn't be doing much of that "feminist stuff." Johnson remembers thinking, "You just wait and see."

Later that fall, while teaching a class of about fifty seminarians, Johnson noticed that students' heads were turning toward the window in the classroom door. She looked to see the face of the dean peeking through with two thumbs up.

Excusing herself from class, Johnson went into the hallway and got the news: "You got tenure." The class heard and "went ballistic," Johnson remembers. Colleagues brought her bouquets of flowers and offered their congratulations.

Years later, when Johnson was preparing her papers for the University of Notre Dame archives, she handed over a large batch of material from the tenure case at Catholic University. Virginia Dowd, the community's archivist, emailed her a few days later: "What is the significance of the cork?" she asked. Johnson later told the story at an annual gala awards ceremony at which she was honored by the Sisters of St. Joseph: "Shortly after I did receive tenure, there was a conference in Washington, DC, that many of our sisters attended. Sister Alice Patricia and Sr. Pat Mahoney filled the bathtub in their hotel room with ice from the hotel's ice machines, and put a whole case of champagne bottles in there on ice. By the time I arrived corks were popping and the celebration of my tenure could be heard around the town. That is the significance of the cork: the profound, festive, over-the-top companionship of the community as I have walked the road of being a theologian. I am ever so grateful."[31]

After it was all over, Johnson would take long walks along the Potomac River, thinking about the church to which she had committed her life and the evil of patriarchy that was threatened by smart women saying challenging things. During the interrogation, she had thought, "In former years they would be lighting the fire outside," to burn her at the stake, Johnson jokes. But this was serious: "Even if you were doing everything right, you could still end up with your livelihood threatened." She considered leaving, but ultimately stayed. Why? "Deep down I still believe in the church, in the Catholic tradition," she says.

Yes, Johnson would stay in the Catholic Church and at the Catholic University of America, for now. Whenever she would get discouraged, she would think of Cardinal Law slamming that binder and dismissing her. It would "get my Irish up," she says. As soon as she could, she applied for a sabbatical and used it to write what she considers her response to the "radicalizing moment" of the tenure battle: *She Who Is*.

CHAPTER FIVE

Disciplined Writer

Sharing with the World

By the late 1980s, the feminist movement had made its way into the church. One Sunday, after a priest at the Catholic University of America called God "Mother" in making the sign of the cross at Mass, a group of theology graduate students stood outside the chapel, debating whether or not such a change was appropriate. Some thought it was refreshing, an affirmation of women's equality before God. Others questioned whether it went too far. In the middle was Beth Johnson.

"My gut feeling at the time was confusion," she recalls about the use of feminine images of the Divine. "I didn't know what I thought. It was new and different, and it both startled and puzzled me. I wasn't saying it was wrong, but neither was I jumping on the bandwagon and saying it was great. I had to figure it out."

Johnson would attempt to "figure it out" during an upcoming sabbatical. Having finally been granted tenure, she was eligible for a year off from teaching to pursue research and writing during the 1988–89 school year. She would use that time to explore the question of feminine language and images for God, the result being *She Who Is*, considered one of the most important books of feminist theology of the twentieth century.

In doing so, Johnson joined other Catholic feminist theologians who were translating the tradition through the lens of women's experience. Mary Daly, considered the founder of Catholic feminist theology, had earlier published her two groundbreaking books: *The Church and the Second Sex* in 1968 and *Beyond God the Father: Toward a Philosophy of Women's Liberation* in 1973, in which she laid out the critique of Christianity's patriarchy. Johnson had read Daly in graduate school, although these books were not assigned by any of her professors. In the next decade came the constructive work in response to the feminist critique. That was done by two pioneering feminist theologians, Rosemary Radford Ruether and Elisabeth Schüssler Fiorenza. In 1983, Radford Ruether, then professor of applied theology at the United Methodist Garrett-Evangelical Theological Seminary at Northwestern University, wrote *Sexism and God-talk: Toward a Feminist Theology*, the first book of systematic theology from a feminist perspective. Schüssler Fiorenza, a professor of theology at the University of Notre Dame at the time, interpreted the gospels through a feminist lens in *In Memory of Her: A Feminist Theological Reconstruction of Christian Origins*. Johnson was "very shaped" by those books, she says.

But patriarchy in the church was not merely an academic issue for Johnson. The tenure battle at Catholic University had opened her eyes to how women could threaten male power in the church. "I thought if *I* threatened them, there is really something wrong," she says, since she saw herself as faithful to the Catholic tradition. "I was determined not to bow to that oppression, but to shed light on it and say it doesn't have to be this way."

By word of mouth, she learned that the Weston Jesuit School of Theology in Boston was a hospitable place for a sabbatical. Not far from Johnson's beloved New York City, Boston offered a rich, intellectual atmosphere in the consortium of theological schools that included Boston College and Harvard University. She was able to meet monthly with other consortium faculty to discuss various academic papers and her own work, and the dean at Weston offered her not only an office but a small, low-rent apartment in one of the Victorian houses then owned by the Jesuits. While she would take the "T" into the city occasionally, for the most part Johnson spent the entire year pursuing the questions that had been percolating inside her for years: Who is this God in whom we believe? Is it possible to envision this God in female form? And what would be the effects if we as a church did that?

While some might find a year of research and writing daunting, Johnson relished the freedom to think and write. "I was like a kid in a candy store," she remembers. "It was like I was born to do this." An early riser, Johnson wakes by 5:00 a.m. without an alarm, makes a cup of tea, spends time in prayer, and begins writing—before even getting dressed or brushing her teeth. "All my books have been written in the morning before the sun comes up," she says.

Johnson avoided distractions while in Boston; only her mother, her superior, and her publisher had her phone number. Although she takes notes by hand when doing library research, by the 1980s, she was writing on a desktop computer, which she had loaded into her car for the trip to Boston. At Catholic University, Jesuit Fr. Ladislas Orsy, the prominent canonical theologian who was two decades older than Johnson, convinced her that using a computer to write was freeing, comparing it to being like a bird flying in the air. "It turned out he was right," she says.

Early notes from 1986 indicate she was struggling with how to phrase the question to focus her writing: Has Mary substituted for God? Can God be imaged as a female? What nuggets could be mined from Mariology for a theology of God? (Johnson's notes also reminded her to "think one hour, write one hour," rather than think for four hours!)[1] While on sabbatical, Johnson originally planned to write a small paperback exploring a few female images in the Bible. "But no book I've written has ended up where I thought it would when I began," she says.

Although her writing process starts with a question, it is then fertilized by wide and deep research. Sometimes that research ends up changing the project, which is what happened with *She Who Is*. Early on Johnson realized she needed to "do theology" and not just repeat what others had done. An insight about the importance of the trinitarian nature of God led her down that path, and although the shift was unexpected, Johnson's integrity required that she follow it. Her "small book" needed to be much more—and it would require an enormous amount of research and new ways of thinking. As a writer, Johnson keeps faithful to her own questions as they evolve. "If you don't find what you're searching for, and you find something else," she says, "you have to go down that path."

For nearly all of her writing career, Johnson has worked with the same editor, Frank Oveis, who is accustomed to her process. That's important, because she refuses to sign a book contract before finishing a manuscript. While most authors, especially prominent ones, receive advance payment and commit to a deadline, Johnson wants the freedom to work on a book "as long as it takes," she says. "Some people take deadlines with a grain of salt, but not me," she says, knowing well that her own hyper-responsibility would require her to finish a book on time. "With something as wonderful as exploring the mystery of God in female form, I couldn't imagine meeting a deadline," she says. So instead she works on the project without a contract until it is completed to her satisfaction.

Oveis remembers Johnson as an "exemplary" author in every way, one whose manuscripts are so well written that he had little work to do. After sending her instructions about the publisher's style, Oveis would scour each manuscript looking for some miniscule thing to correct. "I'd be lucky to find one comma or period out of place," he says, "not to mention her literary style, which is always engaging and often lyrical, very rare in a so-called scholarly book." Later, after his retirement as a senior editor at Continuum Books, Oveis read Johnson's manuscript for *Ask the Beasts*. "Funnily enough, I spent more time on that than I did on any of her other books," he recalls, since his lack of a scientific background led him to ask for clarification on those issues. "I felt good about that, as though I was making up for the little amount of work I ever had to do on her other books," he says. Johnson dedicated *Quest for the Living God* to him.

As Johnson was beginning her writing career, other publishers were courting the new scholar; at least one encouraged her to write a book about Mary. As the first woman to teach theology at Catholic University, Johnson did not want to be stereotyped as a Marian scholar. When she met Oveis (then at the Episcopal publishing house Seabury Press), they hit it off. Born within five days of one another, they were both from lower middle-class, Irish-American families, hers from Brooklyn, his from the Bronx. She had entered the convent after high school; he had spent a decade in the major and minor seminary. "I think the fact that I was gay and open about it also had something to do with my success with

Beth and other women authors," he says, noting they were both members of "semi-oppressed" minorities. Unlike some of the other editors, Oveis encouraged her to write as her first book the one she wanted to—which they both thought (incorrectly, it turns out) would be *She Who Is*.

Johnson wasn't the only feminist theologian writing about feminine images of God, but no one was connecting it to the Catholic tradition as she did in *She Who Is*, especially in the way she used Thomas Aquinas and the Wisdom tradition in the Scriptures to challenge the "idol of the male God," as she calls it. "I knew I was walking a path that others weren't walking yet, and every day was a new discovery," she recalls. Although it was intellectual work, writing *She Who Is* also was a tremendous spiritual experience. "The dividing line between what's intellectual and what's spiritual dissolved," she recalls. "It was like a yearlong discovering of God."

Johnson already had written her doctoral dissertation about the nature of language about God, in which she analyzed—and ultimately disagreed with—Wolfhart Pannenberg's criticism of Catholics' use of analogy. Drawing on another Protestant theologian, Karl Barth, Pannenberg had argued that once a Christian believed in Christ, there was no more need for analogy about God. Instead, Aquinas's belief that Christians need many different analogies to do justice to God's infinite mercy resonated with Johnson, as did Karl Rahner's view of God as mystery. All of this percolated and led to the insight that Christians needed diverse images for God, including feminine ones. Seeing God exclusively or literally as male was detrimental, for women and men, because it limits God, she would argue.

When her research revealed that resistance to feminine images came from patriarchal views of women as inferior and unable to image God, "then it became the justice issue all over again," she says. Occasionally, in the course of writing *She Who Is*, she would remember the scene of her being interrogated by the US cardinals during her tenure battle. "That would spur me on," Johnson recalls. "This would be my way of saying that shouldn't have happened."

Johnson finished that manuscript in 1991 and submitted it to Oveis, but it would not be her first book. The year before her sabbatical, she had been invited by the Catholic bishops of South Africa to deliver a series of lectures on Christology to fifteen hundred clergy and lay leaders of the country. "The whole experience was an immersion in a church struggling to be prophetic disciples of Jesus Christ in the face of the clearly evil policies of their government, policies which have taken an enormous human toll," she wrote about the trip. "I left South Africa reluctantly, having in truth learned more than I taught."[2] Curiously, Durban (South Africa) Archbishop Denis E. Hurley, OMI, who had invited her to South Africa, also wrote a letter in support of her tenure battle at Catholic University. In a letter thanking him, Johnson called Hurley "a kind of 'Amnesty International person' in my case, looking over shoulders of interrogators who knew someone else was watching."[3]

The response to her lectures from the priests in South Africa had been positive, and some asked if they could copy her lecture notes and informally publish them in a small paperback for catechists. Over Christmas during her sabbatical, she received two copies of that book. She was on her way to Brooklyn to give one to her mother when she stopped to have lunch with Oveis at the Grand Hyatt on Forty-Second Street, around the corner from Oveis's office. She showed him the book.

"It was the sorriest book I had ever seen: cheap paper, poor typography, miserable cover," Oveis recalls. He asked to take it home, and Johnson reluctantly agreed; her mother's gift would have to wait. Within a week, he wrote, saying, "You've written your first book."

It needed some revisions, which she made during her sabbatical. She took time out from writing *She Who Is* to revise the lecture notes, taking out the South African references and adding some American ones. She also got permission to include as an additional chapter an article she had written for the journal *Chicago Studies* comparing the Christologies and social justice messages in Pope John Paul II's first encyclical, *Redemptor Hominis*, to the US bishops' letters on peace and the economy.

Consider Jesus was published in 1990 to positive reviews. "Johnson covers an enormous amount of material with remarkable accuracy and clarity,"[4] wrote a reviewer in *The Journal of Religion. Anglican Theological Review* said, "the book could be studied with profit by any inquiring Christian curious as to how the theological wind has been blowing."[5] Johnson indicates in the introduction that the book is meant for those "actively involved in the ministries of the church" and those "seeking greater understanding of their faith."[6] Still in print today, *Consider Jesus* is used as a text in many diaconal programs and college courses.

Of course, reaction to that book was nothing compared to what would come with *She Who Is*. When Oveis first received the manuscript, he was "blown away by [its] broad scope, theological heft, and sheer lyricism," he recalls. "But despite its scholarliness, I felt it would reach a wide market because Christian feminism had reached such a critical mass by then that its success was almost guaranteed." Although written in an academic style, it was still accessible to a wider audience, the so-called "educated layperson." Yet, "very rarely in serious religious publishing does critical and popular success come together in one book," he says. That's exactly what happened with *She Who Is*.

It was initially published to little fanfare. "I just went about my business," remembers Johnson. Slowly, positive reviews began to be written and praise for the book came in. A writer in *Commonweal* called it "prophetic,"[7] while the *Theological Studies* reviewer said it was a "carefully researched, beautifully written, and persuasively argued volume" and "a major contribution to feminist theology."[8]

One April afternoon, while Johnson was working in her office, the phone rang. It was a Dr. David Hester telling her she had won the Grawemeyer Award and that she needed to fly to Louisville the next week for the public announcement. Since she hadn't heard of him or the award, and didn't recall entering her work, she said, "No, thanks. It's the end of the semester, and I'm busy. I can't just take off and go to Kentucky." Deep down, she thought it might have even been a hoax. Hester was disappointed, saying the press was expected to be at the public announcement and that it had been her editor who had nominated her. So Johnson gave Oveis a call and said, "Hey, Frank, do you know anything about this? I told them I couldn't go."

"You told him what? Do you know how much this is worth?" Oveis exclaimed, explaining that with a cash prize of $150,000, the Grawemeyer Award is one of the most lucrative honors in religion. Named for industrialist and philanthropist Charles Grawemeyer, the awards were created with an initial endowment of nine million dollars and are given annually in the fields of education, music composition, religion, psychology, and ideas improving world order by the University of Louisville. The religion award, begun in 1990, is a joint prize from the university and Louisville Presbyterian Theological Seminary.[9] As the 1993 recipient, Johnson was

the first woman and the first Catholic to receive the Grawemeyer Award in Religion. So Johnson called back Hester and
told him she would, indeed, make it to Louisville for the
public announcement the next week.

Rather than honoring lifelong or personal achievement,
the Grawemeyer is unique in that it recognizes ideas instead—and insists that the ideas be understandable to the
general public, not just other academics. The committee
believed Johnson did just that in *She Who Is* by addressing
"a critical issue of spiritual life: How are we to speak rightly
of God in our day? She presents effectively the value of
feminist theology and feminist metaphors for describing
human experiences of the mystery of God."[10]

Six months later, Johnson was back in Louisville for the
official presentation of the award and to give an accompanying lecture the night before. Award winners generally bring
their spouses, but since she didn't have one, Johnson was
accompanied instead by an entire entourage, including her
mother, her godmother, her editor, a member of her religious
community, and a friend. Oveis remembers a visit to Thomas
Merton's hermitage at nearby Abbey of Our Lady of Geth-
semani as another significant part of that trip.

Before the lecture, they had enjoyed an exhibit of women's
art outside under a big tent, with the mayor of Louisville in
attendance. As Hester drove Johnson to the chapel, where
she was going to deliver the lecture, they found themselves
in traffic backed up for miles—caused by the immense crowd
that had showed up to hear her. Hester had to park on the
side of the road and noted that the seminary hadn't had such
a large crowd since a lecture by Fr. Hans Küng, the prominent
and controversial theologian from Switzerland. Two hundred
people were turned away from Johnson's lecture, according
to the local paper, which had also done a feature on her before

the event. "Those who arrived early enough were crammed into pews, crouched in aisles, leaning against walls, even sitting on the 'stage' beside the podium."[11]

Only then did it start to become clear to Johnson how important her book might be to the cause of feminism in the church and in society. "I mean, they weren't Catholic scholars, and here's Thomas Aquinas all over the place," she says. "But I was using scripture in a way that people recognized and appreciated, and [I was] using my own tradition in a way that allowed other people to understand it."

Charles Grawemeyer, who died a month after the 1993 awards ceremony, called Johnson a "deep, deep thinker," saying, "Her work was head and shoulders above the other finalists."[12]

Hester, the director of the religion award, said, "Professor Johnson's argument for the use of feminist metaphors to 'speak rightly of God' is neither strident nor destructive. . . . She reminds readers that language about God is limited and only partially adequate to express the mystery of God."[13]

The Grawemeyer was the first of many awards Johnson would receive for her writing. In 1999, the American Academy of Religion, an interreligious, professional association of nine thousand professors and research scholars from nine hundred colleges, honored Johnson with its Award for Excellence in the Study of Religion for *Friends of God and Prophets*. This was surprising because the organization was at the time perceived as somewhat anti-Catholic, and Johnson's book was about the communion of saints, a very Catholic idea.

In 2004, after the publication of *Truly Our Sister*, Johnson was busy collecting three separate honors from Catholic professional societies. The Catholic Theological Society of America (CTSA), which Johnson had headed as president in

1995–96, gave her its highest honor, the prestigious John Courtney Murray Award, while the smaller College Theology Society also honored her. (Both organizations would later publicly support Johnson during the controversy over *Quest for the Living God*.) The Catholic Library Association also gave her the Jerome Award for outstanding contribution and commitment to excellence in scholarship. Two years later she was the first recipient of the Monika K. Hellwig Award for outstanding contributions to Catholic intellectual life from the Association of Catholic Colleges and Universities.

The amount of attention to Johnson's work is not a fluke, nor is it the result of luck, explains Hilkert, her friend and colleague who says she has read everything Johnson has published and much of the writing that she has not. Hilkert has used *Consider Jesus* in her own teaching for more than twenty years and regularly uses other work of Johnson's—not because she's a friend but because of its quality. She is especially impressed with the way *She Who Is* "builds a footbridge between the classical tradition and feminist insights" as well as its succinct summary of feminist theology in the first chapter.

While some successful authors flit from one editor or publisher to another, looking for higher royalties, increased sales, or more visibility, Johnson is loyal, having stayed with Oveis until his retirement. When the Crossroad and Continuum imprints—yoked for years through multiple corporate owners—finally went their separate ways, Oveis took his employment with the newly independent Continuum. *Consider Jesus* and *She Who Is*, Johnson's two "first-born" books, remained with Crossroad, but their author followed her editor. "Not all my authors took the leap," remembers Oveis. "I was eternally grateful for her loyalty."

Johnson never hounded her publisher for book reviews, sales of foreign rights, or more advertising and marketing.

But neither was she a pushover, especially when it came to the sometimes-contentious discussions about title and cover art. "With Beth's books there was never a question about the title; she hit the bull's eye every time," says Oveis. Cover art was a different matter, with plenty of back and forth between author, editor, and marketing. "I remember one design that had a blue sky and some clouds as a background to suggest transcendence, I suppose," Oveis says. "Beth was apoplectic. To her it suggested heaven or the afterlife in a too literal, spatial sense." Oveis believes the best designs were ones where Johnson found the art herself, as was the case with *Friends of God and Prophets*, *Dangerous Memories: A Mosaic of Mary in Scripture*, and *Ask the Beasts*.

As a tireless public speaker, traveler, and book promoter, Johnson "knows how to sell books," says Oveis. Reviews come fast and furious and are almost always fulsome and laudatory, he says. In addition, foreign publishers are anxious to translate her work, with her books and articles available in more than a dozen languages, including Spanish, German, Portuguese, Italian, French, Dutch, Polish, Icelandic, Lithuanian, Bosnian, Korean, Indonesian, and Thai.

But all of this success was yet to come, as Johnson finished the sabbatical during which she had written most of *She Who Is*. In the fall of 1989, she returned to Catholic University and began teaching, but she already knew in her heart she would be leaving. "I knew I couldn't continue there if I wanted to have a life of pursuing the questions that I had, especially with regard to women," she recalls. "I would always be looking over my shoulder and second-guessing, 'Are they going to come after me again?' " While Johnson had loved her years at CUA, the school had changed. After the controversy and public firing of Fr. Charles Curran, "a dark cloud had come over the place," she says. Johnson consulted her mentors, including Orsy, who advised her to find a place where she could use her voice without fear. That place was no longer Catholic University.

Johnson started talking to friends and putting out feelers to find another graduate theological school that might be looking for someone with her specialties in systematics and Christology. Father Richard McBrien, then chair of the theology department at the University of Notre Dame, wrote and invited her to interview there, with the implication that they would make a place for her if she were interested. But Johnson hesitated. While she respected the school, she could not see herself in South Bend, Indiana. "I'm not a midwesterner," she says. "I could not imagine myself in a place so far from New York." She told McBrien no. Ultimately it was a decision made because of the geography of Johnson's spirituality.

Ironically, her papers did end up in the Midwest, at Notre Dame, in fact. A folder there is full of job offers or requests to apply that she declined over the years, including ones from Georgetown, the University of Chicago, Loyola University Chicago, Boston College, Harvard, and Vanderbilt, even Mundelein Seminary near Chicago and a Methodist seminary in Ohio.[14]

Her job search ended when she received a call from Jesuit Fr. James Keenan at Fordham University, who had heard she was looking to move. Fordham had an opening. "Right away, bells went off, because it was New York," close to family, friends, and her religious community, Johnson remembers. She said yes to Fordham. It would be different than Catholic University, which was a freestanding graduate school where all students were studying theology in some way. Fordham is a major university, with two campuses (Lincoln Center and Rosehill in the Bronx), and Johnson would be teaching both undergraduate and graduate students. There would be new colleagues, including ones in other disciplines. It would take some adjusting.

Leaving CUA as a tenured faculty member was unusual and, for Johnson, heartbreaking. But the reaction to her win of the Grawemeyer Award in her first year at Fordham offered confirmation that she had made the right decision. Father Joseph McShane, then the dean of the undergraduate college (now president of the university), threw "a whale of a party" on campus for faculty, Johnson's family, and her religious community. She remembered thinking that if she had still been at CUA, "they would have whispered about it and then shoved it under the rug, and that would have been the end of it." (Eight years later, Johnson refused to accept an award from CUA, saying she could not "in good conscience" accept it because of the university's "failure to honor basic tenets of academic freedom."[15])

In the end, leaving Catholic University was necessary for the freedom to follow her questions as a scholar. In her resignation letter, she wrote, "I make this decision with a heavy heart . . . but the structures of the university's governance and lack of protection they afford for serious intellectual inquiry into many theological questions make this, for me, a necessary one."[16] Decades later, she remembers that she "didn't do it with a lot of joy, but with a sense of commitment to my future and to whatever work God was calling me to do."

CHAPTER SIX

Caring Teacher

Mentoring Students at Fordham

The late afternoon light shines through a triple panel of antique, leaded windows in a seminar room in the lower level of what used to be Fordham University's library, now home to theology faculty and administrative staff. Nine students—five women and four men, graduate students and a few senior theology majors—are seated around a large table, discussing one of religion's big questions: Is God really omnipotent, or all-powerful, and how does this relate to the reality of suffering in the world?

"Should you pray for sun on the day of the church picnic or not?" Johnson asks, posing a question that makes the theological dilemma concrete. Classical Christian theology says, sure, an omnipotent God can act against the laws of nature. In this late spring session of Ecological Theology, Johnson is leading students through three critiques of that teaching, including that of John Polkinghorne, a British scientist and Anglican priest. For him, the laws of nature are not hard and fast. Instead, "the laws of nature are uncertain and gappy," she says. For example, when water boils,

79

it is not written in stone where and when each bubble will come up. This leaves room for divine action. "God steps in there, as a cause, in the gaps of uncertainty," she says, explaining Polkinghorne.

This makes God "a cause among other causes," which is a problem for classical theologians, Johnson points out, weaving in a story about having met Polkinghorne at a conference. Ultimately, it is a question all theologians must come to terms with: What is God's relationship to the world, not only at the time of creation, but today? Johnson has her own ideas, and she wants her students to understand those of the theologians they are reading. But her primary mode of teaching is to ask questions—and to let her students ask questions, too.

One, who is wearing a T-shirt that says "Epistemology = Ontology," asks about her use of the word *gappy*. Johnson uses the question to clarify what Polkinghorne means: "This is not what some call 'God of the gaps,'" she says, which is problematic because "If you say that what you don't understand equals God, but later you understand, then there is no room for God." Polkinghorne's view is that there is "intrinsic uncertainty built into the system" where God can act without violating the laws of nature.

The discussion turns to another Anglican priest and scientist, Arthur Peacocke, who saw creation as *kenosis*, or God's self-emptying. To make sure the students understand, Johnson throws out some questions, but prefaces them politely with, "May I ask . . . ?" The class is a conversation, and while she is clearly the expert, she respects and listens intently to her students. "Keep going," she urges one, "I want to engage you on that." To another, she notes, "That's the third time you've brought up the ethical consequences"—evidence of her close listening. She allows students to ask hard questions, then sometimes sits back and lets them teach one another, smiling quietly when they get it. It is easy to see why she received the Teacher of the Year Award from Fordham's Graduate School of Arts and Sciences and the Professor of the Year Award from the Graduate Student Association.

Lest things get too abstract, each class begins with a student-led presentation about one species; today it was the blue sea slug. And no class would be complete without some references to Johnson's beloved Aquinas and Rahner, and some mention of feminist critique. This week, it is how an emphasis on self-emptying and self-sacrifice can be seen as reinforcing women's submission to men, as feminist theologian Valerie Saiving has pointed out. Students' heads nod as they scribble furiously in their notebooks. Earlier, she says, "I thought it would be fun to go back to a critique of Thomas Aquinas," then launches into a summary. A student asks, "Is that you, or was that Aquinas?" to which she responds, "A blend. It's my interpretation of Aquinas in light of this critique."

While students respect Aquinas, Johnson is why many theology graduate students come to Fordham. She is a big name in the field whose work is respected and attracts future theologians who want to study with her. Master's and doctoral students tend to gush with language usually reserved for rock stars or love interests when talking about her. "I've found her to be absolutely incredible," says Paul Schutz, who is working on his PhD with Johnson as his advisor. "She's aglow with this love of ideas that is really powerful and kind of electric. It draws you to her." Schutz was not planning to study with Johnson when he initially came to Fordham as a master's student, but taking several classes with her was "life changing," he says. "She's flat-out brilliant."

Doctoral student Jim Robinson remembers coming out of a meeting of Johnson's Ecological Theology class, during which she had taught Karl Rahner in a way he found "ground-breaking"—no easy feat, since even Johnson admits it took her awhile to understand the German theologian when she was in graduate school. Robinson turned to a friend and asked what he thought of the class. "I feel like I just prayed for two and half hours," he said. Says Robinson: "She loves theology and loves to see people mature into deeper relationships with these ideas. She's very nurturing in that regard." He continues, "But she's also not going to let you get away with any sloppy or cheap answers. She thinks these things are worth grappling with."

Despite Johnson's reputation, she is not an academic prima donna, as some elite academics can be. Although she is a prestigious, distinguished professor at the university, Johnson rolls up her sleeves and contributes by serving on committees and sharing in other departmental work. "She never holds herself apart from the citizen duties of the university," says Christine Firer Hinze, director of the Curran Center for Catholic Studies at Fordham, who has known Johnson since her days at Catholic University.

"A lot of famous scholars like to hear themselves talk, and they like the undergraduate worship," says the Rev. Kathryn Reinhard, an ordained Episcopal priest who studied under Johnson at Fordham. "Beth is legitimately excited to hear new ideas, even from eighteen-year-old kids who don't know the breadth of her scholarship. For someone in her position in the academy, that's not that common."

In her years as a student, graduate assistant, and personal assistant for and with Johnson, Reinhard not only learned theological principles, she also gained some life lessons, especially from the way Johnson handled herself during the US bishops' criticism of *Quest for the Living God*. Johnson held a meeting for graduate students shortly after the investigation was made public so students could ask questions. Some in the audience were angry and devastated by what they saw as an unfair attack on their professor. Johnson explained that she was trying to fight the impulse to get mad and defensive. "She said, 'If an undergraduate misread my work, I wouldn't write a vitriolic comeback on their paper about how wrong they were. I would try to teach them,' " recalls Reinhard. "That she could approach her response to the bishops as a teaching opportunity—that continues to be remarkable to me."

Johnson also took time at the end of the classes she was teaching to inform students about the conflict with the bishops and allow them to ask questions. "She just put it on the table," remembers Schutz, who was taking a course with Johnson at the time. Students, even the more traditionalist ones, were incredulous at the charges being leveled against her work, since their experience of her in class was that she was passionately committed to the tradition, Schutz says.

Fordham is a prominent player in theological education, thanks in no small part to Johnson, who has shaped the department by being involved in nearly every hiring decision since she arrived in 1991. That first year she also served on a committee that redrafted the graduate program, strengthening the standards for those who were admitted to and graduated from it. She has never served as chair of the department, avoiding administrative offices so she can focus more on her research and writing. But she is clearly seen as the matriarch of the department. She chairs its five-member strategic planning committee, the only elected departmental committee. She regularly receives the most votes in that "blind" election, according to the department chair.

The Jesuit institution, with its commitment to seeking the truth wherever it leads and a related commitment to supporting freedom of conscience, is a good fit for Johnson, especially after her tenure struggles at Catholic University. The Jesuit charism to serve at the "frontiers" while remaining deeply in the heart of the church is consonant with Johnson's work, says Hinze. "One of the great things about her teaching [is that] she demands that students really appreciate the theological and scriptural tradition," says Hinze. "At the same time, she's out there at those 'frontier issues,' where it's dangerous and people can disagree with you. Going on the frontier is risky, but that's what we do as theologians." Fordham has been willing to stand up for Johnson while she does that risky work. Johnson also demonstrates well the Jesuit value of *cura personalis* or "care for the entire, individual person" in her interactions with her students, says Patrick Hornbeck, chair of the theology department.

In addition to having the largest number of undergraduate majors and minors of any Jesuit college or university, Fordham's theology department offers a master of arts degree and a doctorate in theology. Students in the university's Graduate School of Religion and Religious Education also take theology courses in preparation for careers in ministry, counseling, and other fields. The theology doctoral program is meant to prepare scholars, not just teachers of theology, and students must choose one of five fields of study: Bible, Christianity in antiquity, history of Christianity, systematic theology, or theological and social ethics.[1] Johnson teaches primarily in systematics, advising about five dissertations a year.

She takes the mentoring of graduate students very seriously. "They are the future of our field and the future of the church," she says. "My commitment to teaching them is with this view in mind." Johnson is tough; graduate students consistently note that she has no time for people who do not do the work. "I teach in such a way that they can become skilled professionals themselves," Johnson says of her graduate students. "I can't let people get away with slacking on this, because then you're lessening the contribution they should be making when I'm not here anymore."

At the graduate level, theological education is about more than just passing along a block of knowledge. "It's a way of engaging with people that opens their minds and teaches them the skills—like methods of reading text and interpreting Scripture—that helps them contribute to the church's theology going forward," she says. Colleagues say she probably requires more writing in her graduate courses than other faculty, a requirement that has served students well, since many have gone on to writing careers and positions in colleges and universities around the country. Some of her students at Fordham are seminarians, and certainly most of her former students at CUA were, with many now pastors or heads of religious orders. Her most famous former student would have to be Cardinal Luis Antonio Gokim Tagle of Manila, considered by many to be a *papabile* in the 2013 conclave that elected Pope Francis.

Johnson is a teacher in the classroom and a mentor outside it. "I want to encourage [students] in their own lives to be what they can be," she says. "It was what was done for me." An early statement of her teaching philosophy, written at age thirty-four, listed "thorough knowledge of the subject, clarity of thought and expression, and care for and interest in students"[2] as qualities of a good teacher. "In a very basic sense, no one can teach anyone anything, but as a teacher one can motivate, entice, and engage interest so that the student will be encouraged to pursue learning,"[3] she wrote. Also, "a good teacher should be on the way to becoming a great person himself/herself, ie., integrated, continually curious, respectful of others, and possessed of the saving grace of a kindly humor."[4]

According to her students, her kindness and caring are what set her apart from other scholars and teachers. Johnson is "the consummate mentor," says Schutz. "She's not just a teacher. She's someone who's interested in helping everyone develop in every aspect of their lives." For example, she'll ask how a student's relationship is going, or about students' families—all while maintaining appropriate professional boundaries. Many students come to her with personal issues. And her pragmatic side kicks in when students have problems. Reinhard tells of a graduate student from California who could not afford to go home at Easter, despite some serious family issues. Johnson used her own frequent flyer miles to book a flight for the student. When asked if this story is true, Johnson downplays it: "It was a simple thing. I wasn't using the miles, and someone was in need."

One day Robinson, the doctoral student, stopped by her office and found an umbrella with a note on it: "For Jim. Stay dry. Beth." Apparently, she noticed he didn't have one. "That pastoral element is just so strong," he says, recalling how she visited an undergraduate student from one of her general education courses who ended up in the hospital, with family far away. "If she sees a need, she will fill it," he says.

Although teaching undergraduates is a requirement of her position, Johnson says she would choose to do so even if it weren't. "They're so wonderful," she says. "There's this whole world of learning with regard to faith for them that can be truly exciting and enriching." Many of the courses Johnson teaches at the undergraduate level are general education or core ones, such as Faith and Critical Reason or Christ in World Cultures. She also has taught undergraduate courses titled The Historical Jesus and Religion and Ecology and a senior seminar course called Women and Theology.

Her approach with undergraduate students, most of whom are not theology majors, is to get them excited about theological questions. There is a saying in Fordham's theology department: Their job is not to do catechesis or religious education. Teaching the fundamentals of faith is part of theology, but more important is the bringing of a critical stance so that students will ask questions, such as "Why does the church say this?" Johnson says, "Part of the challenge is making it interesting and engaging enough that—for some, despite themselves—there's something interesting in the course for their own lives."

Of course, not all Fordham undergraduates are Catholic, nor are all of them religious. Johnson cannot assume an interest in theology on their part, and some are turned off by the church. Johnson and other faculty often get the students excited about religion again, by teaching Scripture, for example, in a different way than their pastors have. "I've had students in Christ in World Cultures read the Gospel of Mark and say, 'What? Who is this? We never read these stories before!'" Johnson says, adding: "We have wonderful undergraduate teachers at Fordham who teach with an enthusiasm that gets students interested in religion." Hinze has observed that Johnson encourages young Catholic women trying to find their way in the church. "She's really an example of how you can embrace feminist sensibilities and still be at the heart of the church," Hinze says.

Most undergraduates have no idea they are taking a class from one of the preeminent feminist theologians of their time. In fact, Jillian Yoo didn't even know what a feminist theologian was when she signed up for Christ in World Cultures in fall 2014. She had heard that Johnson made class fun and interesting and was a great speaker. Johnson turned out to be one of her favorite professors.

"Some classes, I felt like I just went to church," says Yoo, a business major who hopes to work for a nonprofit organization after graduation. She became passionate about feminist theology and found herself having "Christ-centered" conversations with other students, "because of the way [Johnson] facilitated class discussions so well," Yoo says. She even *enjoyed* writing the midterm and final—practically unheard of for a core class.

Yet Johnson does have a reputation as a strict professor who demands respect. Critics on RateMyProfessors.com, an anonymous teacher evaluation site, call her a "tough cookie," "the most difficult teacher I've ever had," and complain about how strict she is about no cell phones in class.[5] On campus, there is some scuttlebutt that she is not fair to male students, something Hornbeck, as department chair, has never seen substantiated. Such criticism is common among faculty who teach from a feminist perspective, he says. "It is definitely the case that those who are accustomed to privilege of whatever sort often find it difficult to have that privilege questioned," he says.

Ryan Ramsay found Johnson challenging but fair when he was one of only three men in a section of Christ in World Cultures in 2014. "I never felt uncomfortable, and I talked to the two other guys and they didn't either," says Ramsay, who thinks such criticism is likely from students unwilling to do the work she requires. "She's fair," he adds, when asked if Johnson is an easy or hard teacher. "There's never anything on her exams that she didn't say was going to be there."

Ramsay praised Johnson's willingness to entertain other opinions, admitting that he did not always see eye to eye with her. As a business major, he sparred with Johnson on how people in business can follow Christ's teachings. Several months after the class ended, the two were still exchanging emails and forwarding one another articles on the topic. Ramsay found Johnson's lectures clear, the required readings interesting, and the class discussions even more so. "It was very student driven, with her more of a moderator, although she'd step in if she heard something that wasn't factual," he recalls. A self-described "devout Catholic," Ramsay would bring back things he learned in Johnson's class to his less-religiously committed roommates. "It even sparked interest in their heads," he says.

Her teaching has prompted students to start questioning privilege around them. One student, after taking Johnson's class and learning that the way in which God and Jesus are depicted affects the church's theology, looked around campus and realized that all the nativity scenes were of white Holy Families. With Johnson's support, he started a petition for the university to have at least one Holy Family of color. Johnson also supported members of the campus Women's Empowerment group in its controversial performance of *The Vagina Monologues*. The play, which includes frank discussion of women's anatomy and sexuality, was opposed in 2006 by the campus chapter of the Knights of Columbus. Fordham's Ignatian Society decided to hold a campus debate, inviting Johnson as a supporter and Fr. Joseph Koterski, a philosophy professor, as opposed.

In her opening remarks, video-linked into all the dorms and even the cafeteria, Johnson noted that opponents objected to portions of the play that contained material against church teaching. "But consider: It is against the teaching of the church to commit suicide, especially when disappointed in young love, and yet we continue to perform *Romeo and Juliet* at Catholic universities," she said. "It is against the church to engage in unjust war, and yet Shakespeare's *Henry V*, the story [of] that English king's bloody conquest of France, is enacted on Catholic campuses, without protest. If every play that portrayed sinfulness were taken off the boards, there would be little theater left."[6]

Johnson's second point involved the explicit nature of the title. She quoted chapter one of Genesis in which God creates humans—male and female—and declares that creation is good. Extrapolating, she noted, "We could say God created vaginas, and saw that it was good."[7]

This, of course, drew much howling from the audience. Despite pressure from the Cardinal Newman Society, an outside group, Fordham administrators decided to allow the play. On opening night, Johnson and a group of colleagues approached the theater to find protesters, including seminarians who had been bussed in from St. Joseph's Seminary in Dunwoodie, New York, harassing those in line buying tickets. One, a Latino seminarian, carried a banner of Our Lady of Guadalupe. Johnson asked him if he had devotion to Guadalupe; he replied that he did. "Did you know she had a vagina?" she asked him. "I thought he was going to have a heart attack," she later recalled. Johnson and the other faculty called campus security, since outside protesters were not allowed on campus without a permit. The play sold out every night and continues to be performed on campus.

Johnson's graduate assistants, who help teach and grade students in her undergraduate courses, admit she is not the easiest teacher. "Hers is not a class where you can just show up" and do nothing else, explains Kathryn Reinhard, who has observed undergrads who have failed an assignment and gone into Johnson's office crying, come out smiling. The grade won't be changed. "She will be firm: 'This is the grade you earned and deserved,'" says Reinhard. "But then she'll be pastoral. Through that firmness, she'll take care of the rest of you. So those undergraduates leave with their Fs, but they feel better about the world."

There may be some truth that for undergraduates, at least, Johnson connects most strongly with female students who see her as a role model for what women can accomplish. Doreen Bentum had her feminist consciousness raised in a Women and Theology course with Johnson. Before taking that course, "God was a white man with a pot belly and grey hair," says Bentum, a political science and theology double major from Ghana. Now she can imagine God as a woman, or as a hen guarding her chicks. She also began to question the plan her conservative mother had for her, which involved the fastest path to marriage and babies. Her father encouraged her to pursue a career that would help her country, but "I needed to hear it from a woman," Bentum says. When she asked Johnson for a letter of recommendation for law school, she got that—and an hour of counsel. "She told me that I have these gifts and talents, and it would be wrong not to use them," says Bentum. "Hearing that from a woman I really respect and love really inspired me. I attribute so much of who I am and what I'm doing to those moments with her."

Bentum and her friends frequently left Johnson's class "amazed" and needing to debrief over coffee. One class will long remain with her. During one of the final class meetings of Women and Theology, Johnson brought an acorn for each student, comparing the seed to the ideas they had learned in the class. "What matters is that it grows, and you have to help it grow," Johnson said. Tears well up in Bentum's eyes as she tells the story: "It really sums up my time with her," she says. "She handed me something small, but it's something that's going to turn into something very big and powerful. I still have it and look at it, thinking, 'I'm still trying to germinate. I may not see it right now, but it's coming.'"

Johnson sums up her teaching philosophy as simply to love students. "You teach them because you care about them," she says. "That's why you do what you're doing." She applies that same attitude toward junior faculty in the theology department, whom she quickly takes under her wing. Somewhat famous is her unofficial tradition of taking new faculty out to lunch to the faculty dining room, during their first months, in part to get to know them, but primarily to inform them of the department's expectations, especially for tenure and promotion. Michael Peppard, professor of New Testament and Early Christian Studies, remembers his lunch as "among the most important mentorship moments you can ever have happen." Hornbeck recalls his lunch conversation with Johnson as down-to-earth but also very clear in holding him to high standards. Now chair of the department, Hornbeck says one of Johnson's contributions is "to call us all to be the best possible versions of ourselves."

Colleagues agree Johnson takes her role as a mentor to junior faculty seriously, and when pressed to say something negative about her (Johnson's own directive before interviews), some note that she can be a bit "maternal" in that role. Perhaps this is the eldest child and nun in her coming out a bit, says Hinze. "She has this maternal side to her that can be directive," she says. "Not just, 'I'm on your side,' but 'Have you written more articles this year so you can get tenure?' She doesn't shrink from being that way."

"Authoritative though not intimidating," is how Peppard describes her. "The room changes when she enters it because of her charisma and stature," he says. "But she never lords anything over anyone." In fact, in many faculty meetings, she doesn't say a word. "But when she does, of course, we all sit up and make sure we take good note," Peppard says.

One day, after appearing on a national news show, Peppard emailed a link to the video to his colleagues. A few days later, Johnson replied, pointing out positive aspects of his appearance but also noting that she would be dropping in his mailbox a book about something he had gotten wrong. "The expectation would be that I would read that book that she was loaning me from her personal library," Peppard says. "It's always in a spirit of collegial back-and-forth and mentorship. If someone she knows is going to be out in the national media talking about the church, she wants that person to have the best possible information and way of framing the controversial issues."

Nonetheless, Johnson is seen as positive—though perhaps not "warm and fuzzy"—making comments after meetings like, "What a great discussion. People were being so honest!" or "These young faculty are so amazing!" Hinze calls her an "appreciater" of people and life's little joys, whether it is her cat or the trees outside her window. "She's got this positive energy and even sacramental way of looking at the world," Hinze says. "She sees God as operative in all these things, which is why she's such a good theologian and so beloved."

Though at least one colleague said Johnson might be "too nice for her own good" (agreeing to too many speaking engagements, for example), most concur that she is also nobody's fool. Hinze calls her "politically astute, in the best sense," comparing her to a precinct captain. She is perhaps like many women religious of her generation who have had to think strategically to work successfully in institutions. Johnson is good at connecting "big picture" visionary thinking with the practical details, says her colleague Peppard. "There are so many times when meetings get off track, and you're too much in the clouds or too much in the weeds," he says. "She is very gifted at snapping everyone to attention and reminding them not to forget why we're here."

Likewise, in her own work, Johnson is extraordinarily focused, in part out of respect for the vocation she believes God has called her to. She has no interest in writing an autobiography, for instance, choosing instead to use her time to do theology. Others around her also recognize the importance of her work, from her family members to her congregation. When she was hired at Fordham, Sr. Clara Santoro, her superior at the time, advised her to live close to the university, rather than in a convent of Sisters of St. Joseph that would be farther away. "You are supposed to be writing books, not fighting traffic on the Long Island Expressway," she said. Likewise, Santoro sent a check for Johnson to buy a washing machine for her apartment. "You are supposed to be writing books, not watching the clothes go round in a laundromat."[8] Doing theology, not laundry, is Johnson's gift to the world.

CHAPTER SEVEN

Public Intellectual

Handling Controversy with Grace

It is a rainy Wednesday evening in Chicago in the summer of 2015, but the weather has not stopped some one hundred and fifty people from showing up for a lecture as part of the annual Summer Institute at Catholic Theological Union (CTU), the largest Roman Catholic graduate school of theology and ministry in the United States. Furthermore, this is not a free lecture; each attendee paid twenty-five dollars to hear Elizabeth Johnson speak about her latest book, *Ask the Beasts*.

Johnson is introduced by a fellow sister of St. Joseph, Sallie Latkovich, director of the Summer Institute, who shares some of the speaker's background. But few audience members need the details; they are well aware of Johnson and her work. Her topic of caring for creation has been in the news, especially since Pope Francis's encyclical on the environment, *Laudato Si'*, will be released the next week. But the religious women, seminarians, faculty, students, and other Chicago Catholics in the audience likely are as interested in what Johnson has to say about the environment as what the pontiff will.

"Loving the earth must become an intrinsic part of loving God," she tells the crowd, framing the theological question with the words of naturalist John Muir: "Is God's charity broad enough for bears?"[1] Johnson's short answer is yes, God's mercy is broad enough for all of creation, not just for humans. After detailing the historical impediments to a deeper, more expansive trinitarian understanding of God that could support such a shift in Christians' image of God, she turns to the moral issues in the current ecological crisis in which some twenty-three thousand species become extinct each year. The current destruction of life on earth is "profoundly wrong,"[2] a moral failure and sinful, Johnson says. Instead, an intellectual, emotional, and ethical conversion to the earth is necessary. "We have done theology looking in the mirror at ourselves," she says. "Now it is time to look out the window to see that we are part of a bigger world. . . . We haven't a moment to lose."[3]

After taking questions from the audience, Johnson stays until late in the evening, signing books and chatting with fans. It has been a long day: she flew into Chicago's O'Hare Airport from New York around lunchtime, spent most of the afternoon being interviewed by a reporter, and then had dinner with CTU faculty. The next day she will drive to Milwaukee for three days of meetings with fellow academics at the annual Catholic Theological Society of America (CTSA) conference. There, she will present at two workshops, one devoted specifically to *Ask the Beasts*. In between workshops, meetings, and meals with fellow academics, she is on the phone with family members as they prepare to find an assisted living facility for Aunt Barbara. On the flight home she is already thinking about her next public presentation, a workshop on the pope's new encyclical, for the sisters in her congregation in Brentwood.

Johnson's schedule would be daunting for someone half her age, but she seems to have an unending supply of energy for it. This is her vocation: to be a public intellectual. It requires, obviously, connecting with the public, not always easy for an introvert. But she does it. Her speaking schedule is full and includes major addresses all over the world as well as small presentations at parishes. Her lectures abroad have taken her to England, Australia, and Canada, but also to non-English speaking countries such as Mexico, Germany, Italy, Lithuania, Denmark, and Romania. The list of universities where she has spoken reads like the *U.S. News and World Report's* "Best Colleges" list: Harvard, Yale, Vanderbilt, Emory, Notre Dame, MIT. Of course, she has visited scores of Catholic schools—Boston College, Gonzaga, Santa Clara, Fairfield, John Carroll, Loyola Chicago, DePaul, Creighton, St. Louis, Detroit Mercy, Dayton, Marquette, and more—but she also has been invited to address nonreligious schools, too, such as the University of Pennsylvania, and public schools such as the University of Michigan and the University of Connecticut.[4]

She has received fifteen honorary doctorates, all from Catholic institutions in the United States and Canada, but her reach includes people and institutions of other denominations and faiths as well. Her books, including *She Who Is*, are taught in many Protestant seminaries, and she has shared her theological insights in public addresses at Presbyterian, Baptist, and ecumenical seminaries, in addition to many Catholic seminaries. Like any good academic, she maintains membership in scholarly organizations, such as the CTSA, the American Academy of Religion, and the Association of Theological Schools (ATS), serving on committees of those organizations and even as president of the CTSA and ATS. She also publishes in and has served on the editorial board of scholarly journals, including *Religious Studies Review*, *Concilium* (International Journal of Theology), *Theological Studies*, and *Horizons* (Journal of the College Theology Society). Book publishers, such as the University of Notre Dame Press or Westminster John Knox, regularly ask Johnson to review theological manuscripts.[5]

What makes Johnson different from other theologians, however, is her ability to reach a nonacademic audience. Although her books are not light reading (one of her siblings admits to not being able to understand *She Who Is*), educated Catholics interested in their faith can find most of her work accessible. *Consider Jesus* and *Quest for the Living God* were aimed primarily at people studying for ministry, not doctoral students, and she writes regularly for popular Catholic and religious magazines, such as *America*, *Commonweal*, *U.S. Catholic*, *Catholic Digest*, and *Liguorian*. One of her most recent books, *Abounding in Kindness: Writing for the People of God*, is a collection of her essays, lectures, and reflections written for a broader, nonscholarly audience.

"The danger with so many people in the academy is that they write solid academic books that don't address a wider audience," says Charles Curran, who isn't exactly guilty of such narrowness himself. Johnson has mastered reaching that wider audience, while still remaining a respected member of the academic community. Curran believes that comes from her ability to write clearly and well, the results of years of teaching. And she knows her audience. When Johnson was debating whether to include photos in *She Who Is*, Curran advised her "academics don't do that." She went ahead and included them anyway, and Curran admits he was wrong. "Being a public intellectual in the church is a very important role of the theologian," Curran says. "It is her greatest contribution."

In fact, Johnson is high profile enough that Catholics don't even have to read her writing to be influenced by her. Scholars and popular authors write *about* her, priests use her books in their preaching, even documentarians seek her out. *Newsweek* magazine quoted her in a piece about the controversy over the new *Catechism of the Catholic Church* in 1990.[6] The length of her list of public speaking engagements is exceeded only by the list of requests she has had to turn down. She was among the fifty-three notable women featured in the 2009 Library of Congress engagement calendar, entitled "Women Who Dare," pictured in June, on the page following former first lady Lady Bird Johnson.[7]

Of course, discussion of Johnson's work happens in academic circles, too. Doctoral and graduate students from the United States, Ireland, Spain, Canada, and the Netherlands have made Johnson's work the subject of theses and dissertations. Hundreds of Johnson-related academic articles have been published, usually putting her work in dialogue with other theologians, not to mention the multitude of reviews of her books. Johnson warranted an entry in a Polish book about "great theologians of the twentieth and twenty-first centuries," and her work has been the subject of several books. Some are more academic, such as Shannon Schrein's *Quilting and Braiding: The Feminist Christologies of Sallie McFague and Elizabeth Johnson in Conversation*, but others are aimed at a broader audience, such as *Things New and Old*, a collection of essays about Johnson's theology, which was coedited by Phyllis Zagano and Terrence Tilley. "Few academics have the contributions to make that she does," says Tilley, a colleague at Fordham.

Johnson's expansive reach, especially to people in the pews, may have been the source of the trouble she found herself in with the US bishops' Committee on Doctrine in

2011. It is not public knowledge why the committee began investigating her book *Quest for the Living God*; it had been out for nearly four years already and been translated into other languages. Some suspect it was precisely the book's attempt to summarize the kinds of discussions going on in the academy and share them with Catholics who do not take graduate seminars that bothered the bishops. In the formal criticism of the book, the first paragraph mentions how the book "is written not for specialists in theology but for 'a broad audience.' "[8] Other theories say the investigation was sparked by complaints to Rome, or that it was theological difference of opinion on the part of the committee's secretariat, Fr. Thomas Weinandy, OFM Cap.

Certainly, Johnson knew her work had the potential to anger more traditionalist-minded Catholics, including those in the hierarchy. In fact, she was a bit surprised *She Who Is* didn't land her in some hot water; she had predicted as much when she received the Grawemeyer Award. "No attack, so far," she told a newspaper reporter back in 1993. "But the other shoe could still drop."[9] She also received nasty letters, including a spate of mail challenging her views about Mary after the publication of *Truly Our Sister*.[10] In 2009, she received a death threat in the mail at Fordham University and had to file a police report.[11]

But she regularly receives more positive mail than negative, including praise from clergy and bishops. Bishop Raymond Lucker of New Ulm, Minnesota, wrote in 1992 to praise an interview he had read about her. "I just want to thank you for the marvelous contributions you have made to the theological enterprise in this country,"[12] he wrote. Another bishop, Robert Morneau of Green Bay, said he found her work "forceful and nuanced" in a letter to her. "Know that your work is being treasured here in Wisconsin."[13]

In late March of 2011, Johnson had heard a rumor that the bishops might investigate some of her work, but it was ambiguous enough that she easily dismissed it. On Tuesday, March 29, Johnson arrived at her office to a message from the university president, Fr. Joseph M. McShane, SJ, to phone him when she got in. When she returned his call, Johnson was put straight through. It turned out the rumor was correct: McShane had received a call that morning from New York Cardinal Timothy Dolan that the bishops' Committee on Doctrine would be releasing a criticism of *Quest for the Living God*. The story was set to run in *The New York Times* the next day. Dolan wanted to meet with her and McShane that evening.

Johnson's first reaction was to search her memory for what she could have possibly written that caught the attention of the bishops' committee. She felt guilty, even though she wasn't sure for what. She decided that if she had violated or misrepresented church teaching in any way, she would stand corrected and would rewrite that section of the book. While she waited for the early evening meeting with Dolan, she had a busy day in front of her with classes and meetings. In between, she began receiving emails of support from people who had heard the news through the grapevine.

At 5:30 p.m. she headed over to the president's office and waited for Cardinal Dolan to arrive. In an unusual twist of fate, Dolan's driver and personal secretary who accompanied him was a former student of Johnson's, who had credited her undergraduate course with helping him discern his vocation to the priesthood. In the meeting, Dolan, who was at that time the president of the US bishops' conference, told Johnson that he had been unaware of the Committee on Doctrine's pursuit of the matter until an administrative meeting the previous week when the committee asked permission to publish the criticism, Johnson recalls. Since Fordham University was in his diocese, he asked that the committee delay releasing it until he could speak personally with her.

By not approaching Johnson directly, the Committee on Doctrine was ignoring procedures it had previously agreed to follow. In the 1980s, after several incidents in which theologians were criticized without any preliminary dialogue, the CTSA and the Canon Law Society of America formed a joint committee on "Cooperation between Theologians and the Church's Teaching Authority," which ultimately recommended a process called "Formal Doctrinal Dialogue" to resolve doctrinal disputes.[14] That process, with some refining, was approved by the National Conference of Catholic Bishops in 1989 and, although it reserved the right to publish criticism without consultation, it stated: "It is inevitable that misunderstandings about the teaching of the gospel and the ways of expressing it will arise. In such cases, informal conversation ought to be the first step towards resolution."[15]

The executive director for the bishops' Secretariat for Doctrine confirmed that the committee did not follow the guidelines, citing the urgency of the matter and the widespread use of the book. "The bishops felt that, all things being equal, those guidelines should be or can be employed. But when it seems imperative that something needs to be said and said soon, that cannot always be done," Weinandy told the *National Catholic Reporter*. "The book was out there for three years before it was brought to our attention, so I think the bishops were wanting to clarify the situation as quickly as they could."[16] Cardinal Donald Wuerl of Washington, the chair of the bishops' Committee on Doctrine, later said Johnson should have sought an imprimatur, or an official declaration from a bishop that the book could be published, for an "opportunity to engage in dialogue with the bishops concerning the Catholic teaching expressed in the book."[17] However, an imprimatur is not regularly sought by theologians and instead is used mainly for liturgical texts, catechetical textbooks, and books of prayer.

Dolan's brief visit with Johnson and McShane at Fordham once the criticism was already written didn't sufficiently constitute "conversation" for leaders of the CTSA, who later wrote a statement of support of Johnson that was critical of the process. "We are greatly disturbed that the Doctrine Committee did not follow the approved procedures of Doctrinal Responsibilities which advocate that an informal conversation be undertaken as a first step,"[18] the CTSA statement said. The College Theology Society also issued a statement accusing the committee of causing a "fundamental breach" in the call for dialogue in the church and wounding the "entire community of Catholic theologians."[19]

In a letter in response to the CTSA president, Cardinal Dolan defended the committee, saying the guidelines only apply to individual bishops, not the Committee on Doctrine. In that letter, Dolan also confirmed that the bishops' administrative committee, of which he was a member, "unanimously authorized the immediate publication of the statement."[20] Yet, in the meeting with Johnson and Fordham's president, Dolan admitted that he had not read the book and asked her to summarize what was in it, Johnson says. She gave an ad hoc, twenty-minute lecture that seemed to convince the cardinal that the book did not contain errors against Catholic doctrine, she says. He asked for her cell phone number and said he would be contacting Cardinal Wuerl to see if he could hold the release of the public criticism until the committee spoke with Johnson. Dolan never called.

Tellingly, Dolan did ask Johnson to sign the copy of *Quest for the Living God* that she had brought to the meeting and given to him—which she did, in appreciation for his visit, she says. Dolan gave her a copy of the committee's twenty-one-page criticism, which the university president's secretary copied. The statement said the book "contains misrepresentations, ambiguities, and errors that bear upon the faith of the Catholic Church as found in Sacred Scripture, and as it is authentically taught by the Church's universal magisterium."[21] It took issue with both the method and content of the book, concluding that it "does not take the faith of the Church as its starting point," and warning that it "completely undermines the Gospel and the faith of those who believe in the Gospel."[22] Although originally open to correction by the bishops, after reading the statement, Johnson became confused over what seemed to be a misreading—whether inadvertent or willful—of her book.

After Dolan left, Johnson and McShane sat down to strategize. He offered her the services of the university, including its public relations office, which helped prepare statements from both Johnson and McShane. In his, McShane called Johnson a "revered member of the Fordham community" who "approaches her work as a theologian very seriously and looks upon the action that the bishops' conference [took] as an invitation to dialogue —dialogue on both the mission and craft of the theologian, and on the complexity that a serious theologian faces as she or he tries to explain God to the modern world."[23]

When she got home that evening, the first person Johnson called was Sr. Jean Amore, her superior at the time, who offered the community's support and helped her craft her response. (A year later, when the Sisters of St. Joseph honored Johnson at their annual gala, Amore would call Johnson "a friend of God, a prophet for our age, a companion to 'God-questers' around the world, and our deeply loved sister.")[24] To fortify Johnson for the work she faced that night, a Fordham colleague brought her dinner, along with a bottle of scotch. Johnson made the decision not to speak to the press. "I needed to digest this," she recalls. "I didn't want to go into the press and start yelling at the bishops."

In Johnson's statement for the press, she tried to be gracious, saying it was "heartening"[25] for the bishops to pay attention to the subject of the living God and that she was "appreciative"[26] of the portions of the criticism that noted where she was correct. Johnson then tried to describe the book's task, which seemed to have been misread by the bishops in their labeling it as a "critique of the church's faith."[27] In her statement, Johnson wrote: "The book itself endeavors to present new insights about God arising from people living out their Catholic faith in different cultures around the world. My hope is that any conversation that may be triggered by this statement will but enrich that faith, encouraging robust relationship to the Holy Mystery of the living God as the church moves into the future."[28] Next, she addressed the fact that she had not been approached for dialogue: "One result of this absence of dialogue is that in several key instances this statement radically misinterprets what I think, and what I in fact wrote. The conclusions thus drawn paint an incorrect picture of the fundamental line of thought the book develops. A conversation, which I still hope to have, would have very likely avoided these misrepresentations."[29]

And with that, the public firestorm was ignited. The bishops' criticism was posted online by midnight that evening; McShane's and Johnson's statements followed. The story was picked up by secular and religious news outlets, and debates raged in the comment boxes. The next day, Johnson showed up at Patrick Hornbeck's office door, looking rather pale, and said, "I need to ask you something." Very matter of factly, she told him what was happening and asked Hornbeck to go online and see what was being said. Throughout the public controversy, he became the monitor of the blogosphere and the one responsible for keeping track of the book's rising score on Amazon.

Other members of the department and theologians elsewhere also were shocked and disappointed by the whole incident. "When the bishops decided to challenge her way of doing theology, it wasn't just about her, but also about all of those who do theology in the same spirit," says Hornbeck. Shortly after the bishops' criticism became public, Johnson held a meeting for faculty and graduate students, most of whom signed letters of support. Michael Peppard, a Scripture scholar at Fordham, was disappointed both as a scholar and as a Catholic. "It didn't seem to be a good model of how different leaders of the church ought to engage one another," he says, referring to the committee not following its own procedures. Also, "it didn't follow the etiquette of taking the strongest reading of another's argument if you're going to critique it. It didn't always have a dispassionate or even coherent reading of her argument. I felt that it was picking and choosing things to try to take her down." Stephen J. Pope, a theologian at Boston College, told *The New York Times*: "The reason is political. Certain bishops decide that they want to punish some theologians, and this is one way they do that. There's nothing particularly unusual in her book as far as theology goes. It's making an example of someone who's prominent."[30]

Terrence Tilley, a former chair of the theology department at Fordham who had had his own run-in with Weinandy, was appalled by what he imagines could only have been a "willful misreading" of the book. "I was absolutely dumbstruck when they said she had a theory of metaphor and only of metaphor to talk about God," he says. "That's just so plain wrong, it can only be malicious. She has a section on analogy, metaphor, and symbol as ways that people talk in indirect language about God. That they could think she was only talking about metaphor was, to my mind, a willful and malicious reading." What bothered Tilley most was that this was happening to someone who was herself a "charitable reader" of others' work. "She may be the most capacious and gracious scholar I know," he says, remembering how he once accused her of never saying anything mean about anyone. "I have, too," she replied, showing him a footnote in one of her books with a tough-minded response to a former colleague at Catholic University. The footnoted response "wasn't that bad," Tilley recalls.

To this day, Johnson's colleague and friend Mary Catherine Hilkert, OP, of Notre Dame isn't clear on what the committee found troubling in Johnson's work. "I have consistently found her work to build up people's faith and their hope," she says. "The amazing thing is she was and is so faithful. If they think Beth Johnson is spiritually alarming, they don't know who their friends are." Peppard also had a reaction of "They've got the wrong person." Students in her classes are sure to be taught the classical Catholic tradition, "because that's what she fell in love with," says Peppard. For example, the priest from Sri Lanka writing a dissertation on Pope John Paul II would hardly choose the radically liberal professor the bishops made Johnson out to be as his dissertation director, but he did choose the real one. "It's almost as if they imagined some left-wing progressive, off-the-end-of-the-spectrum person," says Peppard. "Those people exist in the church, but she's not one of them."

The criticism had been written by Weinandy, the Capuchin priest who headed the bishops' Secretariat for Doctrine. In 2000, Weinandy had written a book called *Does God Suffer?* in which he used Thomas Aquinas to argue for divine impassibility or God's inability to suffer.[31] In *Quest for the Living God*, Johnson cites contemporary theologians—particularly post-Holocaust Germans such as Jürgen Moltmann, Dorothee Sölle, and Johann Baptist Metz—who had a different view about a suffering God. Johnson lays out the current debate among theologians in the church, and does not take sides, but her inclusion of the chapter "The Crucified God of Compassion"[32] could be construed as support. That chapter also quotes German cardinal Walter Kasper and Swiss priest Hans Urs von Balthasar. "If these men are saying otherwise, I'm in fairly good company," says Johnson, explaining how respected church members had been part of a debate over how to understand divine compassion and suffering. "I myself am still contemplating this question, trying to think through a both-and position, one that would honor the transcendence of God safeguarded in the classical position while at the same time doing more justice to the texts of scripture which portray God as affected by the world,"[33] she wrote to Cardinal Wuerl during the controversy.

Two years later, Weinandy stepped down from the position with the bishops, having issued five public rebukes of prominent theologians during his eight-year tenure and angering many in academic circles. On news of his retirement, a reporter from the *National Catholic Reporter* noted Weinandy's "blunt, dry humor in personal communication," once asking the reporter: "Why do you work for the devil?"[34] To her credit, Johnson does not carry a grudge against Weinandy, whom she says she has never met. "I'm withholding judgment because I really don't know what was going on with him," she says.

Though this controversy was more widely publicized than Johnson's tenure battle at Catholic University, she was in a stronger position two and half decades later. By this time she had written half a dozen books, all of which had been well received in the theological community, and which had won some sort of prize or award. "It felt very different," Johnson says. "When you don't have tenure and you're being criticized, you're very vulnerable because you could lose your job, and therefore your future." This time, her job was not at stake, and even the bishops were not officially censoring her. According to the canon lawyers she hired to assist her, "it was political," she says, "Everyone saw it as a move of reactionary forces at play under Pope Benedict. It was just one more chapter in that historical period that I got caught in."

Her friend Charles Curran, who had faced his own public struggles with the Vatican, became a trusted adviser during the back-and-forth with the bishops' committee. He advised Johnson not to take the slap from the bishops too seriously and to see it in context. "I kept saying, 'Look, Beth, it's nothing, and it's not going to affect you all that much,'" Curran recalls. "The one consequence might be that you might not get any more honorary degrees from Catholic universities, but you have enough of them already." (St. Mary's University of Minnesota would go through with a planned honorary doctor of educational leadership degree that spring, while the Jesuit Fairfield University in Connecticut awarded her an honorary doctorate in 2014— showing that even the one hypothetical consequence Curran could think of didn't come true.)

That the criticism came from a bishops' committee and not the Vatican's CDF meant the consequences were less severe. Weinandy told *The New York Times* that the impetus for the committee's review of the book did not come from the Vatican.[35] Other theologians who had faced criticisms from the Committee on Doctrine, such as Dan Maguire at Marquette and Todd Salzman at Creighton, had not been seriously affected, Curran noted. A year later he would be advising another woman religious, Sr. Margaret Farley, RSM, at Yale Divinity School, whose book on sexual ethics was criticized by the Vatican. Says Curran, "I would assume there is probably a folder on Beth in the CDF, but they've never done anything because she has never dissented from a Catholic Church teaching. Ever."

That is not to say that the criticism didn't affect Johnson. She admits that the whole ordeal was painful, and colleagues and friends could tell. "What was striking to me was the sense that this institution that she had loved was treating her as if she had been disloyal," says Hornbeck. "She was being treated as someone who was a danger to the faith of others. As a woman of deep faith herself, that was something that hurt her more than anything else." That first evening, Hilkert had left a voice mail message when she read about the bishops' criticism. "I wept when I heard your message last night from exhaustion and appreciation of your support," Johnson wrote back. "It's like a little tsunami washing over me. . . . So ugly."

Friends and strangers rallied to support her, and many offered gifts as well as kind words. In those first weeks, more than fifty people called, including Sr. Helen Prejean, Eugene Kennedy, Sr. Theresa Kane, *Commonweal* editor Peggy Steinfels, former students, religious women, and of course reporters. Johnson's office quickly filled with flowers and boxes of chocolates, and her mailbox was crammed with cards and letters, often accompanied with restaurant gift certificates or offers for getaways, one even with an offer to buy her a new mattress for her bed! She received a couple gift certificates for massages, but didn't care for the experience so gave them away. Some made donations to the Sisters of St. Joseph in her name; others offered their Lenten fasts for her. Johnson's graduate students nabbed a hard hat from a Fordham construction site and signed it with encouraging messages such as, "You are a true architect of the future of theology" and "Always keep your head covered when you go into the unknown."[36] Perhaps the best gift was a standing ovation from the three hundred Sisters of St. Joseph the first time she returned to Brentwood after the ordeal.

The letters and notes of support became so overwhelming Johnson had to hire a graduate student to help her respond to them, while retired Sisters of St. Joseph organized them. Many started with, "You probably don't remember me . . ." or "We've never met . . ." or "I know you haven't heard from me in a while . . ." A handwritten note on a Georgia O'Keeffe card from a former student is typical:

> I am sorry that you have to endure this, and my heart goes out to you. I hopefully envision you deriving some small comfort in joining your hero Aquinas in the pit of ecclesial censure. And I feel certain that, as it was for Aquinas, time will validate your work. Your ideas have the power to inspire expected hope, to transform lives, and to empower the struggle for justice. I know this because that is what your ideas have done for me, and I know that I am not alone in that experience. I never really properly thanked you for what you have done for me . . . and for the whole world. So thank you, Beth Johnson, for writing so eloquently about, and embodying in your own gracious, open, honest way, *She Who Is*.[37]

Some voiced their support more publicly, either in the media or by writing the bishops directly. Jesuit Fr. James Martin, writing on *America* magazine's blog on March 31, 2011, called Johnson "one of my favorite theologians" and detailed how many of her books had been significant in his own vocation and spiritual life. "I hope that this recent notification does not deter anyone from reading the books I've mentioned above, which have been of inestimable help to me in my own quest to seek the Living God,"[38] he wrote.

Religious women, especially, rallied around their sister. Dozens of communities wrote official letters of support, as did hundreds of individual nuns. "This is simply a word of thanks for your intellectual curiosity and ability and courage to share your thinking with us who read your work," emailed Sr. Maxine Pohlman, SSND. "You bring light in this bleak midwinter of our church's existence, and I am deeply grateful."[39] The director of communications of the Leadership Conference of Women Religious, which would soon face its own investigation, wrote, "As one who has been deeply moved and inspired by your writings, I am profoundly grateful for your work and terribly saddened to read the criticism. Please be assured of my prayer for you these days, and my hope that you will be able to continue your courageous scholarship that is so desperately needed in these times."[40]

By the end of the semester, Johnson had been both buoyed by the public support but also exhausted by the publicity and distraction. She had already applied for and been accepted a sabbatical the next school year to write a book about theology and Darwin, and she was determined to spend the time she could be doing theology rather than playing games with the bishops. But the controversy wasn't over yet.

Epilogue

"Dear God, please make us dangerous women," pray the dozens of women—and some men—gathered on the steps of St. Peter in Chains Cathedral in Cincinnati. The protest, timed for rush hour, also coincided with the beginning of the annual meeting of the Leadership Conference of Women Religious (LCWR) on August 7, 2012. With signs, buttons, and placards proclaiming "We support our sisters," "LCWR: Leadership we can trust," and "Nuns R Us," the protesters are clearly on the side of the women in what is heating up to be a battle between the male hierarchy and the female nuns in the Catholic Church.[1]

Nationwide protests of support erupted after the Vatican's apostolic visitation, in which all noncloistered communities of women religious in the United States were required to submit documentation about members, ministries, and financial holdings. Many refused, instead sending only their charters, which had already been approved by a Vatican office. On the streets, in letters, and online, American Catholics—many of whom had been educated by women religious—expressed their support of the women and their dislike of what they perceived as "Sister" being picked on by a big, bad bureaucracy. It didn't help that lay Catholics were already fed up with bishops who had concealed and otherwise failed to address the sexual abuse of minors by some priests in their dioceses.

A few years later came the doctrinal assessment of LCWR, which was separate from the apostolic visitation, though the two were easily conflated by Catholics not clear on distinctions between the Congregation for Institutes of Consecrated Life and Societies of Apostolic Life, which initiated the apostolic visitation, and the Congregation for the Doctrine of Faith (CDF), which led the charge against LCWR. That the CDF involved a team of three US bishops further confused the matters. Around the same time, Sr. Simone Campbell of the social justice lobbying group Network began a series of "Nuns on the Bus" tours, calling attention to political issues that affected the poor. In many lay Catholics' minds, all of this was boiled down to "Nuns = good. Bishops = bad." It was an oversimplification, of course, but contained some truth. The nuns were seen as in the trenches, working in soup kitchens, homeless shelters, or with domestic violence victims, while the bishops, seen as wearing their gold cuff links, living in mansions, and employing personal drivers, issued proclamations questioning the women's devotion.

The criticism of Elizabeth Johnson's *Quest for the Living God* happened during this seven-year, early-twenty-first-century period of hierarchal inquests into religious women, and perhaps some of her supporters saw it as just another unfair attack on a nice nun. In the end, the incident had implications for all theologians, men and women, lay, vowed, or even ordained. But the controversy over the book was not to be Johnson's only part in this period of ecclesial concern about independent-minded women religious.

In 2011, after the initial explosion in the media over the bishops' Committee on Doctrine's criticism of *Quest for the*

Living God, things had settled down a bit for Johnson as she tried to focus on the end of the semester. Meanwhile, others were taking up her cause. In mid-April a statement signed by 180 Fordham faculty members of all ranks, representing 34 departments and programs, proclaimed "unconditional support for our colleague" to the USCCB. "Professor Johnson has made internationally recognized and deeply valuable contributions to her students, to her university, to her field, and to her church community," the statement said. "We urge the USCCB to take steps to rectify the lack of respect and consideration your actions have shown for Sr. Johnson, both as a scholar and as a dedicated woman religious who has given a lifetime of honorable, creative, and generous service to the Church, the academy, and the world."[2]

Father Thomas Weinandy, the executive director for the bishops' Secretariat of Doctrine, replied to the theology faculty with a letter that said the doctrine committee "takes seriously your concerns" and that it "in no way calls into question the dedication, honor, creativity, or service" of Johnson.[3] Johnson received her own letter from Weinandy expressing the "willingness of the Committee to receive any written observations that you may wish to provide with regard to its statement."[4] Johnson says her canon lawyers believed it was "driving them crazy" that Johnson had not responded to the bishops. So she did—in thirty-eight, carefully worded pages, which she titled, "To Speak Rightly of the Living God." (The statement to which she was responding was only twenty-one pages.)

"*Quest for the Living God* is a work of theology. It is not a catechism, nor a compendium of doctrine, nor does it intend to set out the full range of church teaching on the doctrine of God," she wrote. "It appears that part of the present difficulty stems from the Statement's reading my book as if it belonged to a genre other than theology. Theological research does not simply reiterate received doctrinal formulas but probes and interprets them in order to deepen understanding."[5] After the introduction to Johnson's response, ten sections discussed each issue in the bishops' statement, quoting Scripture, the Catechism of the Catholic Church, and Pope John Paul II in defending the appropriateness of theologizing about a suffering God or feminine images of God. In an accompanying cover letter, Johnson referenced St. Athanasius's words during the heated debates of the Council of Nicaea in 325 AD: "I hope in these observations to discuss the matter with you as sister with brothers, 'who mean what we mean, and dispute only about the words.'"[6]

Johnson was clear in her defense of the book, but tried to be respectful in her approach. Her own pacifist beliefs had prevented her from engaging in a public fight with the bishops; her teacher's instincts made her want to explain, rather than rebut. "I would not have written [the response] if they had not asked me to respond," Johnson says, "I took it as a good sign that they were trying to have dialogue. I was wrong." The committee received Johnson's response the week before their national meeting in June. A letter from Cardinal Wuerl thanked her for the document and indicated they would reply after it was reviewed carefully.[7] That "response to her response" came in October, and for the most part, repeated the criticisms in the committee's previous statement. *Commonweal* magazine's headline on the news said: "Committee on Doctrine repeats itself."[8]

Cardinal Wuerl had sent Johnson a copy of this "response to her response," along with a letter indicating he was open to meeting in person.[9] The document, however, was already written and scheduled to be released to the media in two weeks, so it was unlikely any in-person meeting would be of any consequence. The deliberations were clearly over. Wuerl's office sent that letter to Johnson at her Fordham University address, where it sat in her mailbox for weeks, since she was on sabbatical, working at home.

Three days before the document was made public, Wuerl's assistant contacted Johnson via email, repeating the openness to an in-person meeting. Johnson felt like she needed time to digest the document before meeting, and, frankly, was disappointed the meeting was an afterthought, not part of a consultative process. She responded that she would like to take up Wuerl on his offer after letting "the dust settle a bit."[10] That same day, the bishops released their statement and Wuerl was quoted in a press release as saying he offered three times to meet her and that "Sr. Johnson did not respond to any of the offers."[11]

News outlets detailed the back and forth accusations about who offered to meet whom or not, but by now Johnson was tired of it. Her canonical, spiritual, and professional advisers had convinced her any further response was not worth her time or energy. She remembers thinking, "I don't know what your game is, but I'm not playing it because it's not good for my soul and not what I want to do with my mind." And, by then, she was champing at the bit to really commit to her research on Darwin. Inspired by a colleague, she wrote one last response in the form of a lament. "I am responsible for what I have said and written, and stand open to correction if this contradicts the faith," she wrote. "But I am not willing to take responsibility for what *Quest* does not say and I do not think."[12]

Then she let it go. And she heard nothing, for more than two years.

Around Christmas 2014, LCWR contacted Johnson with the news that she had been chosen for the organization's leadership award, which she agreed to accept the following summer. Two months before the awards ceremony, while attending a graduate seminar at Fordham with Cardinal Walter Kasper of Germany, whom Johnson had studied with at Catholic University, someone passed her a note that said, "Here we go again." She later learned that Cardinal Gerhard Müller of the CDF, which was overseeing the investigation of LCWR, had publicly criticized the organization for giving an award to "a theologian criticized by the Bishops of the United States because of the gravity of the doctrinal errors in that theologian's writings," calling it "a rather open provocation against the Holy See and the Doctrinal Assessment."[13] Johnson was not named, but everyone knew Müller was referring to her.

Again, Johnson chose not to engage in a public battle in the media—a decision that was less a strategic tactic and more the practice of her spiritual belief in nonviolence. Those values go back to her involvement in the civil rights and anti-Vietnam War movements and were confirmed by Nelson Mandela's commitment to reconciliation after his imprisonment in South Africa. A longtime admirer of Pax Christi, Johnson regularly attends the New York chapter's Good Friday Stations of the Cross for justice and takes seriously the organization's commitment to resolve differences peaceably. And she hates television shows in which pundits yell at each other. "Responding in kind to violence or bullying just makes the whole thing escalate," she says, noting that she still teaches undergraduate students the Rev. Martin Luther King Jr.'s "Letter from a Birmingham Jail," which lays out the principles of nonviolence. "Everybody I admire in an ethical sense chooses a peaceable means of resolving differences," Johnson says.

LCWR did not back down, and two months later, Johnson was in Nashville to accept the award in front of hundreds of women religious—and the media. She had spent all summer on her brief speech, and it had been vetted by her "posse" of colleagues and friends, as well as the then president of LCWR and other highly placed heads of religious orders. After thanking LCWR for the award and all the religious women who had supported her in what she called "her vocation within a vocation," she reflected on her work as a theologian, especially as one dedicated to "bringing women's voices to the table."[14]

Halfway through the speech, she brought up Cardinal Müller's criticism, then proceeded to trace the historical, sociological, and ecclesiological frameworks that have resulted in the criticism of her book, LCWR, and the award she was receiving that evening. "It appears to me that a negative reaction to works of theology that think in new terms about burning issues has become almost automatic in some quarters," she said. This negative judgment gets repeated, taken for granted, and becomes institutionalized, yet it is vague enough to make it difficult to adequately address, she noted. [15]

She praised LCWR for modeling a different type of leadership. "To a polarized church and a world racked by violence, your willingness to stay at the table seeking reconciliation through truthful, courageous conversation has given powerful witness," she said. "This is costly. . . . Nevertheless, under duress, you persist, giving honest, firm voice to your wisdom gained by years of mystical and prophetic living, as [LCWR president] Pat Farrell said last year. What a grace for our time."[16]

Johnson concluded her story by explaining a photograph that was at the center of each table at the awards ceremony, one she had taken while in South Africa in 1987, when that country was still under apartheid. On a concrete wall, next to a window covered with bars, were the words "HANG MANDELA" in all-caps, black graffiti. But penciled in between the two painted words was the tiny word *on*. "This completely subverts the message!" Johnson said, "To see the resilience of the human spirit under threat of harm (the pencil writer could have been arrested), to watch how an imaginative person turned a curse into a blessing—this has humbled, delighted, and inspired me ever since."[17] The original photo sits on the middle of her desk, in her extremely neat office, at Fordham.

"On" could summarize Johnson's determination, since she was a little girl, to pursue not only a career as a theologian but the mysterious God that is at the heart of that academic discipline. She hasn't always been perfect in her desire to remain completely peaceable (the first draft of her response to the US bishops' committee was "smoking off the page!" she admits), but she has worked hard to maintain a sense of integrity in the face of much public criticism. She has written that dissent can be seen as "one of the truest forms of service and loyalty to the church,"[18] but believes that it, like everything, must come out of love, as modeled by God. "The victory is won not by the sword of a warrior god but by the awesome power of compassionate love by which the living God enters into solidarity with those who suffer in order to heal and set free."[19] When faced with criticism, she remembers to "think back into the roots of who I think I was called to be," she says.

What she has been called to be is a theologian: to think, write, teach, and lecture publicly on the meaning of faith in the face of new questions. "I get paid to think and talk about God,"[20] is how she summed it up in an article. And many of the "new questions" of her generation have clearly been about women. "For the first time in history, theology is now also women's work,"[21] she wrote. During her lifetime, she has witnessed three "tectonic shifts" in theology: from a Roman, clerical, singular way of doing theology, to one that is American (including Latin American), lay (including women), and pluralistic (including ecumenical and inter-religious).[22] Thinking back to her childhood dream of becoming a tugboat driver when she grew up, a friend noted that perhaps her dream had come true. "Women's theology is a tugboat, pushing mightily to get the Church, the bark of Peter, into proper channels regarding the needs of our time," she wrote, reflecting on the idea. "And I am a driver."[23]

She does not let criticism of her work by some in the hierarchy define her; instead she tries to put it in context. "I have learned to see it as part of the culture wars in the church, with right wing bishops trying to cut off certain ways of thinking. Add the gender filter, and it is a situation of men trying to silence a woman. Bishops have tried to silence men too; there is a whole sorry, centuries-long history of anti-intellectual fear in the church, especially among the hierarchy," she says. "I see some bishops' public criticisms of my work as one thread in the tapestry of my life. They add a certain color. But there are ever so many more colors that go to create the overall picture."

Like LCWR, Johnson has tried to model a different type of leadership in the church, one that courageously stands up for what is right, but does so in a collaborative, nonadversarial way that has been a hallmark of many women's religious orders throughout history. Her first book after the controversies from the US bishops and Cardinal Müller, *Ask the Beasts*, was dedicated to LCWR, all communities of St. Joseph sisters, and to her own congregation. In that book, she "got her voice back,"[24] as she told a reporter, in part because of all the affirmation she received, which more than outweighed the criticisms. The investigation of LCWR was abruptly ended in 2015, under the more pastoral Pope Francis. Neither Johnson nor LCWR leaders ever received apologies.

Johnson has become a symbol, something she has never wanted to be. If that had to happen, she is glad it happened later in life, when she was more grounded in who she is. One night while watching a twenty-fifth anniversary performance of *Les Miserables* on PBS, she found herself in tears during the song "Who Am I?" in which the singer answers, "I am Jean Valjean!" "It was so powerful," she says, "That's who I am: Beth Johnson. Whoever's criticizing me, it doesn't matter. I have to be who I am."

Johnson replied to every person who wrote her in the aftermath of investigation of *Quest for the Living God*, often signing her responses, "Still questing . . ." She doesn't regret writing that book and still believes it represents her vision of the exciting theology that is happening in our time. When she was just beginning her theological studies, Johnson's Old Testament professor described Abraham being called to go forth to a new land, setting out on an adventure, chasing the ever-receding horizon. "The spiritual quest sounded so thrilling and worthwhile," she remembers.

Around the same time, with Vatican II still in session, Johnson read a book that would forever influence her. *Your God Is Too Small: A Guide for Believers and Skeptics Alike*, by J. B. Phillips, opened her mind and heart to a bigger, Bible-based view of the Divine, one that she hears reflected in Pope Francis's call for "mercy without bounds." While retirement from teaching will most likely happen someday, Johnson plans to keep writing. For that bigger God, she will always be questing.

Notes

Introduction—pages 1–10

1. Frac Rode, "Statement of the Prefect of the Congregation of Institutes of Consecrated Life and Societies of Apostolic Life, Card. Frac Rode, C.M., on the Apostolic Visitation of Institutes of Women Religious in the USA," November 3, 2009. http://www.apostolicvisitation.org/apvisit/en/news/CardRodeMsg.html.

2. Congregation for the Doctrine of the Faith, "Doctrinal Assessment of the Leadership Conference of Women Religious," April 18, 2012. http://www.vatican.va/roman_curia/congregations/cfaith/documents/rc_con_cfaith_doc_20120418_assessment-lcwr_en.html.

3. Elizabeth A. Johnson, *Quest for the Living God: Mapping Frontiers in the Theology of God* (New York: Continuum, 2007), 4.

4. Elizabeth A. Johnson, Commencement speech (Academy of St. Joseph, New York, June 1980), Elizabeth A. Johnson Papers, Box 1, File 9, University of Notre Dame Archives, Notre Dame, IN.

5. The Bonhoeffer quote from his July 16, 1944, letter to Eberhard Bethge is included in Dietrich Bonhoeffer, *Letters & Papers from Prison,* enlarged edition (New York: Collier, 1972), 360.

6. Phyllis Zagano and Terrence W. Tilley, ed., *Things New and Old: Essays on the Theology of Elizabeth A. Johnson* (New York: Crossroad, 1999), 123.

Chapter One: Eldest Child: Growing Up in Brooklyn—pages 11–21

1. Elizabeth A. Johnson, "Our Annual Christmas Pageant" program, Elizabeth A. Johnson Papers, Box 1, File 3, University of Notre Dame Archives, Notre Dame, IN.

2. Elizabeth A. Johnson, 2014 Outstanding Leadership Award video script, August 15, 2014.

3. Elizabeth A. Johnson, Danforth Fellowship application, personal statement, February 3, 1977, Elizabeth A. Johnson Papers, Box 1, File 10, University of Notre Dame Archives, Notre Dame, IN.

4. Baby book of Elizabeth Ann Johnson, Elizabeth A. Johnson Papers, Box 1, File 1, University of Notre Dame Archives, Notre Dame, IN.

5. Ibid.

6. Virginia Therese Johnson, Magazine article, *Maryknoll* magazine, October 1987, Elizabeth A. Johnson Papers, Box 1, File 4, University of Notre Dame Archives, Notre Dame, IN.

7. Ibid.

8. Mary Agnes Donovan Reed, "Elizabeth Ann," poem in a self-published book, *Samplings*.

9. Baby photo, Elizabeth A. Johnson Papers, Box 1, File 1, University of Notre Dame Archives, Notre Dame, IN.

10. Report cards, Elizabeth A. Johnson Papers, Box 1, File 1, University of Notre Dame Archives, Notre Dame, IN.

11. School award, Elizabeth A. Johnson Papers, Box 1, File 2, University of Notre Dame Archives, Notre Dame, IN.

12. John Cashmore to Elizabeth A. Johnson, Letter, February 20, 1959, Elizabeth A. Johnson Papers, Box 1, File 2, University of Notre Dame Archives, Notre Dame, IN.

Chapter 2: Young Nun: Becoming a Sister of St. Joseph—pages 22–33

1. Elizabeth A. Johnson, Danforth Fellowship application, personal statement, February 3, 1977, Elizabeth A. Johnson Papers, Box 1, File 10, University of Notre Dame Archives, Notre Dame, IN.

2. Elizabeth A. Johnson to Sr. John Raymond McGann, Letter, June 3, 1980, Elizabeth A. Johnson Papers, Box 1, Unnumbered file between 14 and 15, University of Notre Dame Archives, Notre Dame, IN.

3. Sisters of St. Joseph of Brentwood website, https://brentwoodcsj.org/about-us/.

4. U.S. Federation of St. Joseph Sisters website, http://www.sistersofsaintjosephfederation.org/.

5. Jay P. Dolan, *The American Catholic Experience: A History from Colonial Times to the Present* (Garden City, NY: Doubleday, 1985), 437–38.

6. Elizabeth A. Johnson to Sr. John Raymond McGann, Letter, June 3, 1980, Elizabeth A. Johnson Papers, Box 1, Unnumbered file between 14 and 15, University of Notre Dame Archives, Notre Dame, IN.

7. Brentwood College record transcript for Elizabeth A. Johnson, Elizabeth A. Johnson Papers, Box 1, File 4, University of Notre Dame Archives, Notre Dame, IN.

8. Brentwood College commencement program, October 25, 1964, Elizabeth A. Johnson Papers, Box 1, File 2, University of Notre Dame Archives, Notre Dame, IN.

9. Elizabeth A. Johnson, "Worth a Life—A Vatican II Story," in *Vatican II: 50 Personal Stories*, William Madges and Michael Daley, eds. (Maryknoll, NY: Orbis Books, 2003, 2012), 200–204.

10. Pope Paul VI, *Gaudium et Spes* (Pastoral Constitution on the Church in the Modern World), December 7, 1965, http://www.vatican.va/archive/hist_councils/ii_vatican_council/documents/vat-ii_const_19651207_gaudium-et-spes_en.html.

11. Johnson, "Worth a Life—A Vatican II Story."

Chapter 3: Budding Scholar:
Teaching and Learning after Vatican II—pages 34–46

1. Pope Paul VI, "Second Vatican Council II Closing Speech," December 8, 1965, http://www.papalencyclicals.net/Paul06/p6closin.html.

2. Elizabeth A. Johnson, Remarks at Sisters of St. Joseph awards gala, October 25, 2012.

3. Father Eugene H. Maley, St. Mary's Seminary, Norwood, OH, to Elizabeth A. Johnson, Letter, Elizabeth A. Johnson Papers, Box 1, File 6, University of Notre Dame Archives, Notre Dame, IN.

4. Elizabeth A. Johnson, Danforth Fellowship application, personal statement, February 3, 1977, Elizabeth A. Johnson Papers, Box 1, File 10, University of Notre Dame Archives, Notre Dame, IN.

5. Ibid.

6. Ibid.

7. Elizabeth A. Johnson, Comps Exam Sheet, July 31, 1969, Elizabeth A. Johnson Papers, Box 1, File 6, University of Notre Dame Archives, Notre Dame, IN.

8. Elizabeth A. Johnson to "John and Phil, Jim, Therese, Belle, Bernie, Mike and Bill," Private correspondence, Elizabeth A. Johnson Papers, Box 1, File 7, University of Notre Dame Archives, Notre Dame, IN.

9. Ibid.

10. Notes from students in Old Testament course, Academy of St. Joseph, Elizabeth A. Johnson Papers, Box 1, File 7, University of Notre Dame Archives, Notre Dame, IN.

11. Teaching evaluation of Elizabeth A. Johnson, Academy of St. Joseph, November 27, 1970, Elizabeth A. Johnson Papers, Box 1, File 7, University of Notre Dame Archives, Notre Dame, IN.

12. Elizabeth A. Johnson, Private correspondence, Elizabeth A. Johnson Papers, Box 1, File 7, University of Notre Dame Archives, Notre Dame, IN.

13. Ibid.

14. Elizabeth A. Johnson, "Statement of Purpose," Application to the Catholic University of America, Spring 1977, Elizabeth A. Johnson Papers, Box 1, File 10, University of Notre Dame Archives, Notre Dame, IN.

15. Alice McVey to Elizabeth A. Johnson, Letter, June 29, 1977, Elizabeth A. Johnson Papers, Box 1, File 10, University of Notre Dame Archives, Notre Dame, IN.

Chapter 4: Awakened Feminist: Finding Her Voice at CUA—pages 47–63

1. M. Theresa Kane, Text of papal greeting, October 7, 1979, http://www.sturdyroots.org/PDFs/VOC/VOC_Kanepdf.pdf.

2. Elizabeth A. Johnson to Sr. John Raymond McGann, Personal correspondence, October 10, 1979, Elizabeth A. Johnson Papers, Box 1, File 11, University of Notre Dame Archives, Notre Dame, IN.

3. Ibid.

4. Ibid.

5. Ibid.

6. Ibid.

7. Elizabeth A. Johnson to her mother, Personal correspondence, Elizabeth A. Johnson Papers, Box 1, File 11, University of Notre Dame Archives, Notre Dame, IN.

8. Avery Dulles, Career services recommendation for Elizabeth A. Johnson, Elizabeth A. Johnson Papers, Box 1, File 10, University of Notre Dame Archives, Notre Dame, IN.

9. Elizabeth A. Johnson, Note scribbled on folder with Catholic University of America comprehensive exam questions, Elizabeth A. Johnson Papers, Box 1, File 10, University of Notre Dame Archives, Notre Dame, IN.

10. Mary Catherine Hilkert, Remarks in "Tributes to Elizabeth A. Johnson, C.S.J., Recipient of the 2014 Outstanding Leadership Award of the Leadership Conference of Women Religious," August 14, 2014.

11. Elizabeth A. Johnson, Remarks at Sisters of St. Joseph awards gala, October 25, 2012.

12. Carl J. Peter, Career services recommendation for Elizabeth A. Johnson, October 14, 1980, Elizabeth A. Johnson Papers, Box 1, File 10, University of Notre Dame Archives, Notre Dame, IN.

13. Elizabeth A. Johnson to Sr. John Raymond McGann, Letter, June 3, 1980, Elizabeth A. Johnson Papers, Box 1, Unnumbered file between 14 and 15, University of Notre Dame Archives, Notre Dame, IN.

14. Ibid.

15. Ibid.

16. Ibid.

17. Ibid.

18. Ibid.

19. Ibid.

20. Elizabeth A. Johnson, "The Marian Tradition and the Reality of Women," *Horizons*, vol. 12 (1985): 116–35.

21. Luis Antonio G. Tagle to Elizabeth A. Johnson, Letter, October 6, 1986, Elizabeth A. Johnson Papers, Box 4, File 1, University of Notre Dame Archives, Notre Dame, IN.

22. David Power, Letter, September 18, 1986, Elizabeth A. Johnson Papers, Box 4, File 1, University of Notre Dame Archives, Notre Dame, IN.

23. Elizabeth A. Johnson, Remarks at Sisters of St. Joseph awards gala, October 25, 2012.

24. Ibid.

25. "Concerns of the Bishops of the CUA Board With Regard to The Writings of Sister Elizabeth Johnson," August 11, 1987, Elizabeth A. Johnson Papers, Box 4, File 1, University of Notre Dame Archives, Notre Dame, IN.

26. Elizabeth A. Johnson, Note, August 26, 2012, Elizabeth A. Johnson Papers, Box 4, File 1, University of Notre Dame Archives, Notre Dame, IN.

27. Elizabeth A. Johnson, Notes on meeting with CUA bishops over tenure question, September 25, 1987, Elizabeth A. Johnson Papers, Box 4, File 1, University of Notre Dame Archives, Notre Dame, IN.

28. Ibid.

29. Ibid.

30. Ibid.

31. Elizabeth A. Johnson, Remarks at Sisters of St. Joseph awards gala, October 25, 2012.

Chapter 5: Disciplined Writer: Sharing with the World—pages 64–78

1. Elizabeth A. Johnson, Personal notes, 1986, Elizabeth A. Johnson Papers, Box 1, File 14, University of Notre Dame Archives, Notre Dame, IN.

2. Elizabeth A. Johnson, "South Africa: Faith and Apartheid," no date, Elizabeth A. Johnson Papers, Box 7, File 1, University of Notre Dame Archives, Notre Dame, IN.

3. Elizabeth A. Johnson to Bishop Denis E. Hurley, Letter, November 2, 1987, Elizabeth A. Johnson Papers, Box 2, File 11, University of Notre Dame Archives, Notre Dame, IN.

4. Terence J. Martin, "Consider Jesus," *The Journal of Religion*, vol. 72, no. 4 (October 1992): 608–10.

5. Charles C. Hefling Jr., "Book Reviews," *Anglican Theological Review*, 73.3 (1991): 343.

6. Elizabeth A. Johnson, *Consider Jesus: Waves of Renewal in Christology* (New York: Crossroad, 1990), ix.

7. Dennis Doyle, "Critics' Choices for Christmas," *Commonweal*, 119, no. 21 (1992): 27.

8. John H. Wright, Book reviews, *Theological Studies,* 54, no. 2 (1993): 371.

9. Grawemeyer Awards website, http://grawemeyer.org.

10. Ibid.

11. Dianne Aprile, "A Full House," *The Courier-Journal*, November 14, 1993, Elizabeth A. Johnson Papers, Box 3, File 16, University of Notre Dame Archives, Notre Dame, IN.

12. Dianne Aprile, "In God's Name," *The Courier-Journal*, October 24, 1993, Elizabeth A. Johnson Papers, Box 6, File 18, University of Notre Dame Archives, Notre Dame, IN.

13. *The Power of Ideas, Volume I: The University of Louisville Grawemeyer Awards*, 227–29, Elizabeth A. Johnson Papers, Box 6, File 17, University of Notre Dame Archives, Notre Dame, IN.

14. Various letters to Elizabeth A. Johnson, Elizabeth A. Johnson Papers, Box 2, File 9, University of Notre Dame Archives, Notre Dame, IN.

15. Elizabeth A. Johnson to Dean Raymond F. Collins, the Catholic University of America, Letter, January 25, 1999, Elizabeth A. Johnson Papers, Box 3, File 24, University of Notre Dame Archives, Notre Dame, IN.

16. Elizabeth A. Johnson, Resignation letter to the Catholic University of America, April 17, 1991, Elizabeth A. Johnson Papers, Box 2, File 3, University of Notre Dame Archives, Notre Dame, IN.

Chapter 6: Caring Teacher: Mentoring Students at Fordham—pages 79–94

1. Fordham University website, theology department page, http://www.fordham.edu/info/21597/graduate.

2. Elizabeth A. Johnson, Danforth Fellowship application, personal statement, February 3, 1977, Elizabeth A. Johnson Papers, Box 1, File 10, University of Notre Dame Archives, Notre Dame, IN.

3. Ibid.

4. Ibid.

5. "Elizabeth Johnson: Fordham University-Rose Hill" entry, Rate MyProfessors.com, http://www.ratemyprofessors.com/ShowRatings.jsp?tid=220981.

6. Elizabeth A. Johnson, "Reflections on *The Vagina Monologues*," February 27, 2006, Elizabeth A. Johnson Papers, Box 2, File 8, University of Notre Dame Archives, Notre Dame, IN.

7. Ibid.

8. Elizabeth A. Johnson, Remarks at Sisters of St. Joseph awards gala, October 25, 2012.

Chapter 7: Public Intellectual: Handling Controversy with Grace—pages 95–112

1. Heidi Schlumpf, "Is God's Charity Broad Enough for Bears" (blog post), *National Catholic Reporter,* June 11, 2015, http://ncronline.org/blogs/ncr-today/gods-charity-broad-enough-bears.

2. Ibid.

3. Ibid.

4. Elizabeth A. Johnson, Curriculum vitae, long form, 2015.

5. Ibid.

6. Kenneth Woodward, "Revolt against Rome?" *Newsweek*, vol. 115, no. 12 (March 19, 1990): 74, Elizabeth A. Johnson Papers, Box 10, File 2, University of Notre Dame Archives, Notre Dame, IN.

7. Video script, "Elizabeth A. Johnson, C.S.J., 2014 LCWR Outstanding Leadership Award," August 15, 2014.

8. Committee on Doctrine, United States Conference of Catholic Bishops, "Statement on *Quest for the Living God: Mapping Frontiers in the Theology of God*, by Sister Elizabeth A. Johnson," March 24, 2011, United States Conference of Catholic Bishops website, http://www.usccb.org/about/doctrine/publications/upload/statement-quest-for-the-living-god-2011-03-24.pdf.

9. Dianne Aprile, "In God's Name," *The Courier-Journal*, October 24, 1993, Elizabeth A. Johnson Papers, Box 6, File 18, University of Notre Dame Archives, Notre Dame, IN.

10. Various letters, Elizabeth A. Johnson Papers, Box 10, File 12, University of Notre Dame Archives, Notre Dame, IN.

11. Anonymous postcard to Elizabeth A. Johnson, November 9, 2009, Elizabeth A. Johnson Papers, Box 3, File 30, University of Notre Dame Archives, Notre Dame, IN.

12. Raymond A. Lucker to Elizabeth A. Johnson, Letter, April 21, 1992, Elizabeth A. Johnson Papers, Box 9, File 11, University of Notre Dame Archives, Notre Dame, IN.

13. Robert F. Morneau to Elizabeth A. Johnson, Letter, March 14, 1996, Elizabeth A. Johnson Papers, Box 3, File 30, University of Notre Dame Archives, Notre Dame, IN.

14. Joint Committee of the Canon Law Society of America and Catholic Theological Society of America, "Doctrinal Responsibilities: Procedures for Promoting Cooperation and Resolving Disputes between Bishops and Theologians" (Appendix 1), *Canon Law Society of America Proceedings* 45 (1983): 261–84.

15. National Conference of Catholic Bishops, "Doctrinal Responsibilities: Approaches to Promoting Cooperation and Resolving Misunderstandings between Bishops and Theologians," NCCB Document, June 17, 1989.

16. Joshua J. McElwee and Thomas C. Fox, "Bishops Ignored Own Guidelines in Johnson Critique," *National Catholic Reporter*, April 7, 2001.

17. NCR staff, "Johnson: Bishops' condemnation came without discussion," *National Catholic Reporter*, March 31, 2011.

18. Catholic Theological Society of America Board of Directors, "Response of the Board of Directors of the Catholic Theological Society of America to the Statement on *Quest for the Living God: Mapping Frontiers in the Theology of God,* by Sister Elizabeth A. Johnson, Issued by the Committee on Doctrine, United States Conference of Catholic Bishops, March 24, 2011," April 8, 2011.

19. Joshua J. McElwee, "US Bishops to Replace Staffer behind Theological Investigations," *National Catholic Reporter*, January 30, 2013.

20. Timothy M. Dolan to John E. Thiel, Letter, July 7, 2011.

21. Committee on Doctrine, Statement on *Quest for the Living God.*

22. Ibid.

23. Joseph McShane, University statement, March 31, 2011, Elizabeth A. Johnson Papers, Box 11, File 6, University of Notre Dame Archives, Notre Dame, IN.

24. Jean Amore, Remarks at 2012 gala honoring Elizabeth Johnson, October 25, 2012.

25. Elizabeth A. Johnson, "Elizabeth Johnson's Response" [to US bishops' Committee on Doctrine Statement], March 30, 2011, *America* magazine website, http://americamagazine.org/content/all-things /elizabeth-johnsons-response.

26. Ibid.

27. Committee on Doctrine, Statement on *Quest for the Living God.*

28. Elizabeth A. Johnson, "Elizabeth Johnson's Response."

29. Ibid.

30. Laurie Goodstein, "Bishops Criticize Nun's Book," *The New York Times*, March 30, 2011.

31. Thomas G. Weinandy, *Does God Suffer?* (Notre Dame, IN: University of Notre Dame Press, 2000).

32. Elizabeth A. Johnson, *Quest for the Living God: Mapping Frontiers in the Theology of God* (New York: Continuum, 2007).

33. Elizabeth A. Johnson, "To Speak Rightly of the Living God: Appendix," July 11, 2011, Elizabeth A. Johnson Papers, Box 11, File 2, University of Notre Dame Archives, Notre Dame, IN.

34. McElwee, "US Bishops to Replace Staffer."

35. Goodstein, "Bishops Criticize Nun's Book."

36. Elizabeth A. Johnson, Personal notes, Elizabeth A. Johnson Papers, Box 11, File 9, University of Notre Dame Archives, Notre Dame, IN.

37. Maggie Meier to Elizabeth A. Johnson, Personal card, June 8, 2011, Elizabeth A. Johnson Papers, Box 11, File 18, University of Notre Dame Archives, Notre Dame, IN.

38. James Martin, "The Case of Sister Elizabeth Johnson" ("In all things" blog post), *America*, March 31, 2011, http://americamagazine .org/content/all-things/case-sister-elizabeth-johnson.

39. Maxine Pohlman to Elizabeth A. Johnson, Email, March 30, 2011, Elizabeth A. Johnson Papers, Box 11, File 19, University of Notre Dame Archives, Notre Dame, IN.

40. Annmarie Sanders to Elizabeth A. Johnson, Email, March 31, 2011, Elizabeth A. Johnson Papers, Box 11, File 19, University of Notre Dame Archives, Notre Dame, IN.

Epilogue—pages 113–22

1. Video, August 7, 2012, Cincinnati, "Nun Justice Project," http://nunjustice.tumblr.com/.

2. Faculty of Fordham University to United States Conference of Catholic Bishops, Statement, April 18, 2011, Elizabeth A. Johnson Papers, Box 11, File 6, University of Notre Dame Archives, Notre Dame, IN.

3. Thomas C. Fox, "Bishops' Committee Reaches Out to Catholic Scholars," *National Catholic Reporter,* May 13, 2011, http://ncronline.org/news/faith-parish/bishops-committee-reaches-out-catholic-scholars.

4. Thomas G. Weinandy to Elizabeth A. Johnson, Letter, April 28, 2011, Elizabeth A. Johnson Papers, Box 11, File 2, University of Notre Dame Archives, Notre Dame, IN.

5. Elizabeth, A. Johnson, "To Speak Rightly of the Living God: Observations by Dr. Elizabeth A. Johnson, CSJ, on the Statement of the Committee on Doctrine of the United States Conference of Catholic Bishops about her book *Quest for the Living God: Mapping Frontiers in the Theology of God,*" published in "Origins," Catholic News Service, vol. 41, no. 9 (July 7, 2011).

6. Ibid.

7. Donald Wuerl to Elizabeth A. Johnson, Letter, June 22, 2011, Elizabeth A. Johnson Papers, Box 11, File 2, University of Notre Dame Archives, Notre Dame, IN.

8. Grant Gallichio, "Committee on Doctrine Repeats Itself," *Commonweal*, October 28, 2011, https://www.commonwealmagazine.org/blog/committee-doctrine-repeats-itself.

9. Donald Wuerl to Elizabeth, A. Johnson, Letter, October 11, 2011, Elizabeth A. Johnson Papers, Box 11, File 2, University of Notre Dame Archives, Notre Dame, IN.

10. Adam Park [secretary to Cardinal Donald Wuerl] to Elizabeth A. Johnson, Email correspondence, October 25–26, 2011, Elizabeth A. Johnson Papers, Box 11, File 2, University of Notre Dame Archives, Notre Dame, IN.

11. Donald Wuerl, Press release, October 28, 2011, Elizabeth A. Johnson Papers, Box 11, File 2, University of Notre Dame Archives, Notre Dame, IN.

12. Elizabeth A. Johnson, "Johnson: Bishops' Latest 'Paints Incorrect Picture' of Book" and statement of October 28, 2011, *National Catholic Reporter*, http://ncronline.org/news/johnson-bishops-latest-paints-incorrect-picture-book.

13. Grant Gallichio, "CDF Prefect Tells U.S. Nuns They Were Wrong to Honor Elizabeth Johnson," *Commonweal*, blog post, May 5, 2014, https://www.commonwealmagazine.org/blog/cdf-prefect-tells-us-nuns-they-were-wrong-honor-elizabeth-johnson.

14. Elizabeth A. Johnson, Leadership Conference of Women Religious Remarks for Leadership Award Dinner, Nashville, TN, August 15, 2014, LCWR website, https://lcwr.org/sites/default/files/calendar/attachments/elizabeth_johnson_csj_response_-_8-15-14_1.pdf.

15. Ibid.

16. Ibid.

17. Ibid.

18. Elizabeth A. Johnson, "Dissent in and for the Church," LCWR newsletter, June 1986, Elizabeth A. Johnson Papers, Box 6, File 13, University of Notre Dame Archives, Notre Dame, IN.

19. Elizabeth A. Johnson, "And Their Eyes Were Opened: The Resurrection as Resource for Transforming Leadership," CMSM/LCWR Joint Assembly, Anaheim, California, August 1995, Elizabeth A. Johnson Papers, Box 6, File 14, University of Notre Dame Archives, Notre Dame, IN.

20. Elizabeth A. Johnson, "A Theologian for the 21st Century," *Liguorian* (April 2004): 21–23, Elizabeth A. Johnson Papers, Box 6, File 15, University of Notre Dame Archives, Notre Dame, IN.

21. Ibid.

22. Elizabeth A. Johnson, "Tectonic Shifts: Catholic Theology as American, Lay, and Pluralistic," *Horizons: The Journal of the College Theology Society*, vol. 26, no 2 (Fall 1999), 295–98.

23. Elizabeth A. Johnson, "A Theologian for the 21st Century."

24. Jamie Manson, "With Book on God and Darwin, Elizabeth Johnson Gets Her Voice Back," *National Catholic Reporter*, February 13, 2014, http://ncronline.org/blogs/grace-margins/book-god-and-darwin-elizabeth-johnson-gets-her-voice-back.

Bibliography

Primary Sources

Johnson, Elizabeth A. "The Marian Tradition and the Reality of Women." *Horizons* 12 (1985): 116–35.

———. "Dissent in and for the Church," LCWR newsletter (June 1986).

———. *Consider Jesus: Waves of Renewal in Christology.* New York: Crossroad, 1990.

———. *She Who Is: The Mystery of God in Feminist Theological Discourse.* New York: Crossroad, 1992.

———. *Friends of God and Prophets: A Feminist Theological Reading of the Communion of Saints.* New York: Continuum, 1998.

———. "Tectonic Shifts: Catholic Theology as American, Lay, and Pluralistic." *Horizons: The Journal of the College Theology Society* 26, no. 2 (Fall 1999): 295–98.

———. *Truly Our Sister: A Theology of Mary in the Communion of Saints.* New York: Continuum, 2003.

———. "Worth a Life," in *Vatican II: 50 Personal Stories*, edited by William Madges and Michael Daley, 200–204. Maryknoll, NY: Orbis Books, 2003, 2012.

———. "A Theologian for the 21st Century." *Liguorian* (April 2004): 21–23.

———. *Dangerous Memories: A Mosaic of Mary in Scripture.* New York: Continuum, 2006.

————. *Quest for the Living God: Mapping Frontiers in the Theology of God*. New York: Continuum, 2007.

————. "Elizabeth Johnson's Response." *America* magazine website, March 30, 2011, http://americamagazine.org/content/all-things/elizabeth-johnsons-response.

————. "To Speak Rightly of the Living God: Observations by Dr. Elizabeth A. Johnson, CSJ, on the Statement of the Committee on Doctrine of the United States Conference of Catholic Bishops about her book *Quest for the Living God: Mapping Frontiers in the Theology of God*." *Origins* 41, no. 9 (July 7, 2011).

————. "Johnson: Bishops' Latest 'Paints Incorrect Picture' of Book." *National Catholic Reporter*, October 28, 2011, http://ncronline.org/news/johnson-bishops-latest-paints-incorrect-picture-book.

————. *Ask the Beasts: Darwin and the God of Love*. London: Bloomsbury, 2014.

————. Leadership Conference of Women Religious Remarks for Leadership Award Dinner, Nashville, TN, August 15, 2014, https://lcwr.org/sites/default/files/calendar/attachments/elizabeth_johnson_csj_response_-_8-15-14_1.pdf.

Zagano, Phyllis, and Terrence W. Tilley, ed. *Things New and Old: Essays on the Theology of Elizabeth A. Johnson*. New York: Crossroad, 1999.

Unpublished interviews by Heidi Schlumpf

Bentum, Doreen. April 20, 2015, Fordham University, New York, NY.

Bia, Margaret Johnson. August 4, 2015. Telephone.

Cavanaugh, Sister Karen. June 9, 2015. Telephone.

Curran, Charles. July 1, 2015. Telephone.

Hilkert, Mary Catherine. July 30, 2015. Telephone.

Hinze, Christine. April 20, 2015, Fordham University, New York, NY.

Hornbeck, Patrick. April 20, 2015, Fordham University, New York, NY.

Johnson, Elizabeth A. January 13, 2015. Telephone.

———. February 20, 2015. Telephone.

———. March 5, 2015. Telephone.

———. April 20, 2015, Fordham University, New York, NY.

———. June 10, 2015, Catholic Theological Union, Chicago, IL.

———. June 30, 2015. Telephone.

———. July 21, 2015. Telephone.

———. August 5, 2015. Telephone.

———. August 14, 2015. Telephone.

Johnson, Susan. February 17, 2015. Telephone.

Oveis, Frank. August 8, 2015. Email.

———. August 11, 2015. Email.

Peppard, Michael. April 20, 2015, Fordham University, New York, NY.

Ramierez, Jean Hostetter. February 16, 2015. Telephone.

Ramsay, Ryan. April 20, 2015, Fordham University, New York, NY.

Reinhard, Kathryn. April 20, 2015, Fordham University, New York, NY.

Robinson, Jim. April 20, 2015, Fordham University, New York, NY.

Schutz, Paul. April 20, 2015, Fordham University, New York, NY.

Tilley, Terry. April 20, 2015, Fordham University, New York, NY.

Yoo, Jillian. April 20, 2015, Fordham University, New York, NY.

Index

Abby of Our Lady of
    Gethsemani, 73
Academy of St. Joseph
    (Brentwood), 39–40
Aldrin, Buzz, 36
Amazon.com, 106
America, 98, 111
American Academy of Religion,
    74, 97
Amore, Sister Jean, CSJ, 104–5
Anthanasius, Saint, 116
Andre, Sister Margaret, CSJ, 17
Anglican Theological Review,
    71
Anselm, Saint, 4
Apartheid, 119–20
Apostolic visitation (of US
    women religious), 3, 113–14
Armstrong, Neil, 36
Association of Catholic
    Colleges and Universities, 75
Association of Theological
    Schools (ATS), 97
Atlantic Ocean, 7, 18
Aquinas, Thomas, 3, 45, 69, 74,
    81, 107, 111

Barth, Karl, 35, 51, 69
Benedict, Pope, 109
Bentum, Doreen, 91–92
Bernardin, Joseph, 59–61
Bia, Margaret (Peggy) Johnson
    (sister), 11, 12, 16, 17, 23,
    24, 29–30
Bible Today, The, 37
Bonhoeffer, Dietrich, 7, 35
Boston, 47, 59, 60, 66
Boston College, 41, 66, 77, 97,
    106
Brentwood College, 28, 30,
Brooklyn, 5, 11–21, 68, 70

Campbell, Simone, 114
Canon Law Society, 102–3
Cardinal Newman Society, 90
Carter, Jimmy, 47
Catechism of the Catholic
    Church, 99, 116
Catholic Digest, 98
Catholic Library Association, 75
Catholic Theological Society of
    America (CTSA), 74, 96, 97,
    102–3

Catholics for Equality, 47

Catholic Theological Union, 95–96

Catholic University of America, The, 118; doctoral studies, 5, 41–46, 50–52; Pope John Paul II visit, 47–50; faculty member at, 52–63; tenure battle, 5, 56–63, 65, 70, 76–78, 84, 108–9

Cavanaugh, Karen, CSJ, 28–29

Chicago, 47, 59, 77, 95–96

Chicago Studies, 71

Cincinnati, 113

Civil Rights Movement, 31, 36–37, 118

College Theology Society, 56, 75, 103

Collins, Judy, 36

Commonweal, 72, 98, 110, 116

Concilium, 98

Congregation for the Doctrine of the Faith (CDF), 3, 57, 59, 109–10, 114, 118

Congregation for Institutes of Consecrated Life and Societies of Apostolic Life, 3, 114

Coney Island, 15

Congar, Yves, 35

Continuum Books, 68, 75

Cooperation between Theologians and the Church's Teaching Authority (joint committee), 102–3

Council of Nicaea, 116

Creighton University, 97, 109

Crossroad Publishing, 75

Curran, Charles, 42, 53, 58–59, 76, 82, 98, 109–10

Daly, Mary: *Beyond God the Father*, 65; *Church and the Second Sex*, 65

Danforth Foundation Scholarship, 37

Darwin, Charles, 3, 8, 112, 117

de Duras, Felicite, 26

de Lourdes, Joan, CSJ, 41, 52, 57

De La Salle Christian Brothers, 35

DePaul University, 97

Des Moines, Iowa, 47

Detroit, 31

Detroit Mercy University, 97

Discernment: to enter religious life, 17, 18, 20–21; to teach at CUA, 53–54

Doctoral degree work: applications to schools, 41–43; at CUA, 5, 41–46, 50–52

Dolan, Cardinal Timothy, 101–4

Dowd, Virginia, 62

Dulles, Avery SJ, 42, 49–50, 51, 59

Duval, Leon, 34,

Ecumenism, 38, 61, 121

Emory University, 97

Episcopal Church: ordination of women, 47

Fairfield University, 97, 109

Farley, Margaret, RSM, 110

Farrell, Pat, OSF, 119

Fatula, Mary Ann, OP, 52

Feminine images of God, 2, 8, 60, 64–65, 68, 69, 73–74, 116

Feminism, 15–16, 41, 44–45, 49–50, 58, 64, 87–88, 91

Feminist theology, 24, 44, 53, 56, 61, 65, 71, 73, 75, 80, 81, 87–88, 121

Fiorenza, Elisabeth Schussler, 45, 65; *In Memory of Her*, 65

Fiorenza, Francis, 45

Fitzmyer, Joseph, SJ, 42

Fordham University, 1–2, 77–78, 79–94, 100, 115, 118; Christ in World Cultures course, 86–88; Curran Center for Catholic Studies, 82; Ecological Theology course, 79–82; Graduate School of Arts and Sciences, 81; Graduate School of Religion and Religious Education, 84; Graduate Student Association, 81; Ignatian Society, 89–90; Women's Empowerment group, 89–90; Women and Theology course, 87, 91–92

Forty Hours Devotions, 23

Francis, Pope, 85, 122

Garrett-Evangelical Theological Seminary, 65. *See also* Northwestern University

Gaudium et Spes (Vatican II document), 32–33

Georgetown University, 77

God, 2, 6–8, 66–67, 79–80, 120, 122; "living God," 4, 105, 112, 120; of mystery, 5, 7–8, 10, 105; suffering of God, 108, 116; Trinity, 6, 67, 96

Gonzaga University, 97

Grand Hyatt, 70

Grawemeyer Award, 72–74, 78, 100

Grawemeyer, Charles, 72, 74

Guadalupe, Our Lady of, 90

Habit (religious garb), 38–39

Harvard University, 66, 77, 97

Henry Street Settlement House, 19

Henry V (Shakespeare), 90

Hester, David, 72–74

Hickey, Cardinal James, 57, 59–61

Hilkert, Mary Catherine, OP, 43–45, 75, 107, 110

Hinsches ice cream shop, 18

Hinze, Christine Firer, 82, 84, 87, 92–93

Holy Family, 89

Holy Spirit, 6, 33

Holy Wisdom, 2, 60. *See also* feminine images of God

Hopkins, Gerard Manley, SJ, 28

Horizons, 56, 98

Hornbeck, Patrick, 84, 88, 92, 105, 110

Hugo, Victor, *Les Miserables*, 122

Humanae Vitae (Vatican II document), 37, 58

Hurley, Denis E., OMI, 70

Ignatian *examen*, 5
Inclusive language, 45, 64
International travel, 97; to
    Europe, 51–52; to South
    Africa, 60, 70, 119–20

Jesus, 6, 31, 44, 49, 56, 70, 86,
    89; Christology, 8, 51, 52, 61,
    70–71, 77
John Carroll University, 97
John Courtney Murray Award,
    75
John Paul I, Pope, 46
John Paul II, Pope, 46, 47–49,
    71, 116
Johnson, Elizabeth: *Abounding
    in Kindness*, 98; *Ask the
    Beasts*, 8, 68, 76, 95, 96, 121;
    Consider Jesus, 8, 70–71, 75,
    98; *Dangerous Memories*, 76;
    Friends of God and Prophets,
    8, 74, 76; *She Who Is*, 8, 51,
    63, 65, 67, 69–70, 71–74, 75,
    76, 97, 98, 100; *Truly Our
    Sister*, 8, 56, 74, 100. *See also
    Quest for the Living God*
Johnson, Lady Bird, 99
Johnson, Lyndon B., 32, 37
Johnson, Margaret Reed
    (mother), 14–16, 19, 22, 27,
    29–30, 66, 70, 73
Johnson, Susan (sister), 12, 22,
    29–30
Johnson, Walter (father), 5, 13–
    14, 16, 21–22, 27, 29

Johnson, Virginia Therese, MM,
    14
Journal of Religion, 71
Judaism, 5–6,

Kane, Theresa, RMS, 48–50, 110
Kasper, Walter, 108, 118
Keenan, James, SJ, 77
Kennedy, Eugene, 41, 110
Kennedy, John F., 32
Kennedy, Robert, 37
Kennedy Center, 44
King, Martin Luther King, Jr.,
    32, 37, 118; "Letter from a
    Birmingham Jail," 118
Knights of Columbus (Fordham
    chapter), 89
Komonchak, Joseph, 58, 60
Koterski, Joseph, SJ, 89
Küng, Hans, 51, 73

Language about God, 51, 69,
    73, 74, 107
Latkovich, Sallie, CSJ, 95
Laudato Si' (encyclical), 95
Law, Bernard, 59–61, 63
LCWR, 3, 48, 112, 113, 121–22;
    doctrinal assessment, 3, 114,
    118; Outstanding Leadership
    Award, 5, 117–120
Leo Honor Society, 20
Les Miserables (Hugo), 122
Library of Congress, 99
Liguorian, 98
Liturgical Press, *The Bible
    Today*, 37
Loughlin, John, 26

Louisville, Kentucky, 72–74
Louisville Presbyterian Theo-
   logical Seminary, 72–74
Loyola University Chicago, 77,
   97
Lucker, Raymond, 100

Maguire, Dan, 109
Mahar, Mary, SSND, 48
Mahoney, Pat, CSJ, 62
Mandela, Nelson, 118, 120
Manhattan College, 35–39
Maria, Mother Immaculata,
   CSJ, 35
Marialis Cultus (apostolic letter
   on Mary), 56
Marquette University, 97, 109
Martin, James, SJ, 111–12
Mary, 6, 8, 14, 17, 22, 48, 56,
   57, 58, 59, 61, 67, 68, 100
Massachusetts Institute of Tech-
   nology (MIT), 97
Master's degree work, 35–38
McBrien, Richard, 77
McCarthy, Eugene, 37
McGann, John Raymond, CSJ,
   49, 54, 57–58
McShane, Joseph, 78, 101, 103,
   104
Merton, Thomas, 73
Metz, Joann Baptist, 108
Milwaukee, 96
Missionary Cenacle Apostolate,
   18–19
Moltmann, Jurgen, 35, 108
Monika K. Hellwig Award, 75
Morneau, Robert, 100–101

Mount Manresa (Jesuit retreat
   house, Staten Island), 13
Muir, John, 96
Müller, Gerhard, 118, 119, 121
Mundelein Seminary (Chicago),
   59, 77

Nashville, 118–20
National Catholic Reporter,
   102, 108
National Gallery, 44
National Lutheran/Catholic
   Dialogue, 38, 61
National Shrine of the Immacu-
   late Conception, 47–50
Network (lobbying group), 114
New York City, 47, 66, 77. *See
   also* Brooklyn
New York Times, The, 101,
   106, 109
Newsweek, 99
Nonviolence, 118
Northwestern University, 65
Nostra Aetate (Vatican II docu-
   ment), 38

Ordination of women to the
   priesthood. *See* Priesthood,
   ordination of women
Orsy, Ladislas, 58, 66, 77
Our Lady of Perpetual Help
   Parish and School
   (Brooklyn), 13, 16–17, 26
Oveis, Frank, 67–69, 70–73,

Pannenberg, Wolfhart, 8, 51–
   52, 69

Patriarchy, 62, 65, 69
Patricia, Alice, 62
Paul VI, Pope, 37, 46, 56, 58
Pax Christi, 118
Peacocke, Arthur, 80
Pennsylvania, 53
Peppard, Michael, 92–94, 106, 107
Perfectae Caritatis (Vatican II document), 31
Peter, Carl J., 42–43, 52
Philadelphia, 26, 47
Phillips, J. B., 122; *Your God Is Too Small*, 122
Pohlman, Maxine, SSND, 112
Polkinghorne, John, 79–80
Pontifical Gregorian University (Rome), 41
Pope, Stephen J., 106
Potomac River, 62
Power, David, OMI, 56–57, 58, 60
Prejean, Helen, CSJ, 110
Priesthood, ordination of women, 23–24, 47–50, 61
Psalms, 4, 6

Quest for the Living God, 2, 4–5, 8, 68, 98; controversy with US bishops, 29, 75, 82–83, 99–112, 114–17, 122
Quilting and Braiding (Schrein), 99

Racism, 19, 32, 36–37; Detroit Race riots, 31

Rahner, Karl, 4, 7, 35, 45–46, 51, 69, 81, 82
Ramierez, Jean Hostetter, 18
Ramsay, Ryan, 88–89
RateMyProfessors.com, 88
Ratzinger, Joseph, 58. *See also* Benedict, Pope
Redemptor Hominis (encyclical), 71
Redemptorist priests, 17, 23; Redemptorist brothers, 23
Reed, Barbara (aunt), 15–16, 19–20, 51, 73, 96
Reed, Mary Agnes Donovan (grandmother), 15–16
Reinhard, Kathryn, 82–83, 86, 90–91
Religious Studies Review, 98
Ride, Sally, 54
Robinson, Jim, 81–82, 86
Romeo and Juliet (Shakespeare), 89
Rubsys, Anthony, 36
Ruether, Rosemary Radford, 65; *Sexism and God-talk*, 65

Sabbatical (1988–89), 64–67, 70, 71; (2011–12), 3, 112, 117
Sacred Heart, 14
Sacrosanctum Concilium (Vatican II document), 36
St. Brendan Diocesan High School for Girls (Brooklyn), 18, 20
St. Joseph's Seminary (Dunwoodie, New York), 90

St. John's University (New York), 20

St. Joseph Academy (New York), 5

St. Joseph's College (New York), 26, 41, 53

St. Louis University, 97

St. Mary's Hospital (Brooklyn), 13

St. Mary's University of Minnesota, 109

St. Peter in Chains Cathedral (Cincinnati), 113

Saints, 8, 14, 61,

Saiving, Valerie, 81

Salzman, Todd, 109

Santa Clara University, 97

Santoro, Clara, CSJ, 57, 94

Schneiders, Sandra, 45

Scholar, role of, 7–8, 25, 34, 53–54, 55, 75, 78, 84, 106–7, 115

Schutz, Paul, 81, 83, 86

Scripture, 2, 4, 6, 56, 57, 67, 74, 87, 104, 108, 116, 122; Gospels, 6, 65; Wisdom literature, 6, 69; Book of Job, 8, 36–37, 55; historical-critical method, 40, 85

Seabury Press, 68, 90

Second Vatican Council, 4, 5, 17, 26, 27, 28, 30, 31–33, 34–39, 55, 122

Secret Service, 48

Shakespeare, William, 89–90

Shifra, 57

Sisters of St. Joseph of Brentwood, 6, 17, 21, 22–33, 38–39, 41–42, 53–54, 62, 94, 96, 105, 121; Noviate years, 27–31; final vows, 25, 32–33, 34

Sisters of St. Joseph, US Federation, 26

Social justice, activism, 31–32, 89–90, 118

Society of Jesus (Jesuits), 1, 23, 66, 83–84

Sölle, Dorothee, 108

South Africa, 60, 70–71, 118, 119–20

Stations of the Cross, 23, 118

Steinfels, Peggy, 110

Student Service League, 19

Tagle, Luis Antonio G., 56, 85

Teaching: in elementary schools, 30–31; in high school, 39–40; in colleges/universities, 41, 52–63, 79–84

Teilhard de Chardin, Pierre, 7

Temple Emmanuel (New York), 5–6,

Tenure battle at CUA, 5, 56–63, 65, 70, 76–78, 84, 109. *See also* Catholic University of America, The

Thanksgiving, 9, 19–20

Theologian, role of, 4, 24, 34, 42, 53–54, 55–58, 62, 65, 67, 84–85, 98, 102–3, 104, 119, 120–21

Theological Studies, 72, 98

Things New and Old, 9–10, 99

Tilley, Terrence, 99, 106–7

University Club (Washington, DC), 60
University of Chicago, 77
University of Connecticut, 97
University of Dayton, 97
University of Louisville, 72
University of Michigan, 97
University of Notre Dame, 41, 65, 77, 97, 107; archives, 9, 49, 62, 77; Press, 98
University of Pennsylvania, 97
University of the State of New York Regents Scholarship, 20
US Conference of Catholic Bishops (National Conference of Catholic Bishops), 101, 102, 115; Committee on Doctrine, 2, 99, 101–7, 109–10, 114–17, 120; Secretariat for Doctrine, 100, 102, 108, 115
US bishops letters on peace and economy, 71
U.S. Catholic, 98

Vagina Monologues, 89–90
Vanderbilt University, 77, 97
Vietnam War, antiwar movement, 31–32, 36–37, 118

Von Balthasar, Hans Urs, 108

Weinandy, Thomas, OFM Cap., 100, 102, 106, 108, 109–10, 115; *Does God Suffer?*, 107
Westchester County, 15
Westminster John Knox, 98
Weston Jesuit School of Theology, 66
Wilmington College (Ohio), 20
Women in the church, 48–49, 51, 54, 55–56
Woman theologians, 41, 42–43; WIT (Women in Theology), 44–45,
Women religious, 3, 14, 17–18, 22–33, 38–39, 47–50, 54, 110, 113–14, 118, 121
Women's Ordination Conference, 47
World War II, 13, 36
Wuerl, Donald, 102–3, 108, 116–17

Yale Divinity School, 41, 97, 110
Yoo, Jillian, 87–88

Zagano, Phyllis, 99